THE
UNCONDITIONED
MIND

J. Krishnamurti, circa 1955.

THE
UNCONDITIONED
MIND

J. KRISHNAMURTI AND
THE OAK GROVE SCHOOL

DAVID EDMUND MOODY

QUEST
BOOKS

Theosophical Publishing House
Wheaton, Illinois * Chennai, India

First Quest Edition 2011

Quest Books
Theosophical Publishing House
P. O. Box 270
Wheaton, IL 60187-0270

www.questbooks.net

Cover design by Kirsten Hansen Pott
Typesetting by Prepress-Solutions.com

Cover photograph by Ziegler. Copyright Krishnamurti Foundation of America.

The author acknowledges with gratitude the assistance of the Krishnamurti Foundation of America and the Krishnamurti Foundation Trust, England, in photo research and reproduction permissions.

Library of Congress Cataloging-in-Publication Data

Moody, David Edmund.
The unconditioned mind: J. Krishnamurti and the Oak Grove School / David Edmund Moody.
    p.   cm.
Includes bibliographical references and index.
ISBN 978-0-8356-0894-7
1. Krishnamurti, J. (Jiddu), 1895–1986. 2. Education—Philosophy.
3. Oak Grove School. I. Title.
LB880.K742M66 2011
370.1—dc23   2011019804

Printed in the United States of America

5   4   3   2   *   11   12   13   14   15

For Anita Rose, Leanne, Vivika, and Suzaji…

goddesses all.

CONTENTS

CONTENTS

"We are concerned with the problem of meeting the student, who is already conditioned—parents are conditioned, the educator is conditioned—how to uncondition (hmm?) the mind, so that he is completely, wholly intelligent. Not partially, in a segment which is so small—which is knowledge, the field of knowledge. He is terribly alive, terribly intelligent, terribly cunning there. But the rest is *darkness!*"

—J. Krishnamurti,
speaking to Oak Grove School
parents and staff

The Pavilion at Oak Grove School.

PREFACE

In 1975, the philosopher and educator J. Krishnamurti established an elementary and secondary school in the Ojai Valley, some eighty miles north of Los Angeles. The school was named Oak Grove, and Krishnamurti personally oversaw and guided its development during the last ten years of his life. As a participant in the school, I had the good fortune to witness his involvement at close quarters for a sustained period of time. What follows here is the record of what I observed.

Krishnamurti's philosophy, articulated from a public platform for over fifty years, represents perhaps the most comprehensive exploration ever conducted into the nature and dynamic structure of consciousness. The sheer volume of his recorded talks and dialogues is unparalleled, and the challenge to the individual listener to grasp and assimilate his central insights is direct and fundamental.

George Bernard Shaw, at the end of his long life, was acquainted with Krishnamurti as a young man and declared him to be "the most beautiful human being" he had ever met.

Aldous Huxley formed a close friendship with Krishnamurti and said his teachings were commensurate with those of the Buddha. Theoretical physicist David Bohm devoted much of his life to a collaboration with Krishnamurti and an effort to comprehend the full meaning of his work. Henry Miller, Howard Fast, and many other writers, artists, and intellectuals have acknowledged the truth and beauty of Krishnamurti's teachings. Millions of listeners all over the world have been touched by their exposure to his work.

Krishnamurti's philosophy is not some abstract set of principles designed to answer arcane questions about issues remote from everyday life. Rather, his aim was to explore the actual dynamics of ordinary consciousness and to reveal the sources of conflict and illusion in each individual. His observations encompass the full spectrum of issues associated with daily life, including love, desire, fear, pleasure, conflict, violence, time, knowledge, personal identity, and death.

Central to his outlook is a penetrating examination of the nature of thought and the ways in which it is universally misunderstood. Krishnamurti proposed that a radical revolution in the structure of consciousness is not only possible but imperative, and is brought about through fundamental insight into the thinking process.

Krishnamurti did not confine his exposition of these issues to the public platform or the many published volumes of his talks and dialogues. Over the course of his lifetime, he established several schools whose basic purpose was to cultivate a quality of holistic intelligence, rather than a narrow expertise in academic subjects. His schools were designed to enable students not only to secure a good means of livelihood but to prepare for the whole of life.

Several of these schools were located in India, one was in England, and two in North America. In 1948, Krishnamurti joined forces with Aldous Huxley and others in Ojai to create the Happy Valley School, a boarding school for secondary students. Some ten years later, however, he severed his relationship with Happy Valley.

The Oak Grove School was the last of Krishnamurti's endeavors of this kind. As his youngest child, so to speak, he gave it special attention and did his utmost to ensure the firmness of its foundation and the direction of its growth.

I was the first academic teacher hired at Oak Grove and later served as educational director and as director of the school. I had been a student of Krishnamurti's work for several years and was drawn to the school by my dual fascination with the teachings and with the man who had articulated them. The opportunity to serve the mission he had outlined for the school and to witness the manner of his involvement was irresistible.

Krishnamurti's actual persona, as I observed it over the course of a decade, more than justified my expectations. He was often rather shy and subdued in social settings, but on other occasions, his responses to people and situations sparkled like an iridescent diamond.

My observations of him were not isolated or immune from the currents and challenges of daily life but rather were embedded in the context of the mission of the school. Education in the conventional sense has been concerned with the transmission of traditional values and parochial perspectives. The intent of the Oak Grove School, by contrast, was precisely to free the student from narrow, sectarian patterns of thought. In a radical departure from traditional pedagogy, our aim was to uncondition the mind and so to lay the foundation for a new form of consciousness.

What I did not fully anticipate when I joined the school were the rich mixture of other participants and their competing visions of the essential meaning of Krishnamurti's work. The collective energies of these personalities created a complex field of forces, one whose warp and woof were not easy to navigate. The effort to do so challenged my capacities to the maximum degree. The drama that resulted and Krishnamurti's involvement in it form the essential thread of the narrative that follows.

The intensity of the total experience and the task of assimilating it fully accounts for the time it has taken to produce this report. Only with some distance from the events described was it possible to present them in a balanced perspective. The opportunity for long reflection more than compensates, in my view, for any time lost.

It has become the convention in books on Krishnamurti to use quotation marks for statements purportedly made by him, even when the author only intends to paraphrase or to reconstruct conversations not actually remembered word for word. That temptation is strictly avoided here. Quotation marks are reserved for comments he made that are remembered precisely or with a very high degree of accuracy. Anything less, in my view, does a disservice not only to Krishnamurti but to the reader as well.

In this volume I endeavor to capture my observations and to distill their meaning in as factual and dispassionate a manner as possible. Nevertheless, I was deeply involved in the events that follow, and the opportunity for error or distortion is always present. May the muses allow me to remain true to my own recollections and yet sensitive to the possibility of alternative perspectives. And may I succeed in capturing here in high fidelity the colors and the texture of the man at the center of this work.

Krishnamurti and his brother, Nitya, Ojai, approximately 1922.

CHAPTER ONE

OJAI

Much of the topography of Southern California is the product of colliding continental plates, sliding in opposite directions at the implacable pace of two inches per year. The zone of interaction between the plates is called the San Andreas Fault, and the tensions that accumulate there over the course of millennia are immense. These tensions are responsible for periodic massive earthquakes as well as for more enduring features of the terrain. Some of the mountain ranges and valleys that normally would run in a north-south direction are forced into an east-west configuration. Among these is the Ojai (OH-hi) Valley, some eighty miles north of Los Angeles and fifteen miles inland from the sea.

Because of its orientation, the valley receives a greater quantity of sunlight than it would otherwise, and its slight elevation combines with the sun to produce a Mediterranean climate. For this reason, the valley was at one time considered conducive to the treatment of tuberculosis.

In 1922, two young men came to the Ojai Valley for this purpose. Jiddu Krishnamurti and Nityananda were brothers, twenty-seven and twenty-four years of age, respectively. Nitya had been suffering from the effects of tuberculosis—fever, cough, and progressive weakness—for over a year.

Whenever they appeared in public, the two men were impeccably dressed and groomed. Krishna stood about five feet, seven inches and had the features of a Grecian sculpture: eyes, nose, and mouth were formed with fine regularity and beauty of proportion. His brother was two inches shorter, and his facial characteristics were less classical but almost as appealing in their way: his rounded cheeks and a slight tilt of the head (a consequence of impaired vision in his left eye) suggested a cherubic, somewhat vulnerable quality.

The property where the brothers had been invited to stay was in the far eastern end of the valley, adjacent to the surrounding foothills. Two houses were situated there among a dozen acres of orange groves. Pine Cottage, the smaller house, had a porch and a view of the valley and was flanked by a young pepper tree. Behind the property, a trail ran into the wilderness of Horn Canyon and beyond, all the way up to Topa Topa Bluff, a massive, striated structure a mile above the valley floor.

In a letter to a friend, Nitya described Ojai in these terms:

In a long and narrow valley of apricot orchards and orange groves is our house, and the hot sun shines down day after day to remind us of Adyar, but of an evening the cool air comes down from the range of hills on either side. Far beyond the lower end of the valley runs the long, perfect road from Seattle in Washington down to San Diego in Southern California, some two thousand miles, with a ceaseless flow of turbulent traffic, yet our valley lies happily, unknown and forgotten, for a road wanders in but knows no way out. The American Indians called our valley the Ojai or the nest, and for centuries they must have sought it as a refuge.

The brothers' first few weeks in Ojai were uneventful. The course of Nitya's illness was variable, as usual: at first, his symptoms seemed to stabilize, and he gained both weight and energy; then he coughed up blood again. On the whole, however, the restful setting and dry air of the valley appeared to be having a beneficial effect. He became strong enough to accompany Krishna on the trail behind the property for half a mile or so, where there was a stream with a pool deep enough to wade in up to the hips. The brothers rode horses as well as hiked, and when Nitya was feeling less well, Krishna would read to him for an hour or more each day. Ecclesiastes and the stories of O. Henry were among their mutual favorites.

It was not only Nitya who arrived in Ojai in need of recuperation; Krishna's malaise, however, was psychological in nature. He was suffering from a sense of deep discontent with the whole course of his life and the manner in which he was living it. His education had been a bore, and the career others had charted for him was a source of intense ambivalence.

Krishna regarded the isolation of Ojai as an opportunity to get to the bottom of what was troubling him. After the brothers had settled in, he began to sit in meditation for half an hour each morning and again in the evening. His idea of meditation had nothing to do with mantras or with some ascetic removal from reality. Rather, it consisted of a focused observation of himself—coupled with the intention, as he wrote in a letter to a friend, "to annihilate the wrong accumulations of the past years."

Two weeks after commencing to meditate in this manner, Krishna began to feel tired and restless one evening after dinner.

He complained of a pain in the nape of his neck, and Nitya observed there a knot, as if of a contracted muscle, about the size of a marble. Krishna slept the night through without difficulty, but the discomfort and fatigue resumed the following morning, and he lay down on his bed.

Nitya recorded the events that followed in a long and detailed narrative. He wrote that, "Our lives are profoundly affected by what happened...our compass has found its lodestar."

Also present to witness what occurred were Albert P. Warrington, who was staying on the property with the two brothers, and Rosalind Williams, a nineteen-year-old neighbor who had befriended them. At Warrington's suggestion, Rosalind entered Krishna's room in Pine Cottage and found him lying on his bed, moaning and writhing in pain. The pain appeared to be concentrated in the head, the spine, and the back of the neck. It came intermittently, in waves, and alternated with periods of intense shivering. While shivering, however, Krishna complained of burning heat.

Rosalind approached and tried to calm and comfort him. At times, she was able to hold him and to settle him down somewhat; at other times, he pushed her away. He often seemed only partially conscious; he was by turns coherent and unintelligible. Krishna settled down sufficiently for everyone to eat lunch, but afterward, the pain returned and became so intense that he could not keep his meal down. When nightfall came, he was able to relax somewhat, and again he slept the night through.

During the course of the next day, the symptoms became more acute. Krishna was extremely sensitive to light and noise. The room was kept darkened at his request, and everyone tried to keep all sounds to a minimum; even slight rustlings startled and disturbed him. He settled down again after nightfall, but the process resumed the following morning.

Toward the end of the third day, after the others had finished their evening meal, "[S]uddenly the whole house seemed full of a terrific force," Nitya wrote, "and Krishna was as if possessed."

> He would have none of us near him and began to complain bitterly of the dirt, the dirt of the bed, the intolerable dirt of the house, the dirt of everyone around, and in a voice full of pain said that he longed to go to the woods. . . . Suddenly he announced his intention of going for a walk alone, but from this we managed to dissuade him, for we did not think that he was in any fit condition for nocturnal ambulations.

Mr. Warrington noted that he knew Krishna's bed was perfectly clean, for he had personally changed the linen that morning. Nitya continued:

> Then as he expressed a desire for solitude, we left him and gathered outside on the verandah, where in a few minutes he joined us, carrying a cushion in his hand and sitting as far away as possible from us. Enough strength and consciousness were vouchsafed him to come outside but once there again he vanished from us, and his body, murmuring incoherencies, was left sitting there on the porch. . . .
>
> The sun had set an hour ago and we sat facing the far-off hills, purple against the pale sky in the darkening twilight.

A young pepper tree stood at the entrance to the cottage, "with delicate leaves of a tender green, now heavy with scented blossoms." Warrington suggested to Krishna that he might like to go sit under the tree, and after a moment's hesitation, he did so. Presently, those on the veranda heard a sigh of relief, and Krishna called out to ask why they had not sent him there much earlier. Then he began to chant an ancient song, one familiar to the brothers from their childhood.

A few moments later, according to Nitya, something occurred outside the parameters of ordinary reality. He claimed there was an unusual light in the sky, and he had an overwhelming sense of the arrival of some transcendent personality or intelligence. "The place seemed to be filled with a Great Presence," he wrote, and, "In the distance we heard divine music softly played."

After this evening, the strange process ended. A few days later, Krishna recorded his own impressions of what had transpired:

> There was a man mending the road; that man was myself; the pickaxe he held was myself; the very stone which he was breaking up was a part of me; the tender blade of grass was my very being, and the tree beside the man was myself. I almost could feel and think like the roadmender, and I could feel the wind passing through the tree. . . . I was in everything, or rather everything was in me, inanimate and animate, the mountain, the worm, and all breathing things.

Krishna invoked images of nature to convey what occurred under the pepper tree. His experience there is not easy to correlate with the days of pain and semi-consciousness that led up to it:

> There was such profound calmness both in the air and within myself, the calmness of the bottom of a deep unfathomable lake. Like the lake, I felt my physical body, with its mind and emotions, could be ruffled on the surface but nothing, nay nothing, could disturb the calmness of my soul. . . .

I have drunk at the clear and pure waters at the source of the
fountain of life and my thirst was appeased. Never more could I be
thirsty, never more could I be in utter darkness. I have seen the Light.
I have touched compassion which heals all sorrow and suffering; it is
not for myself, but for the world.

—∿—

At the time he came to Ojai, Krishnamurti's life had been
largely shaped by the guidance of author and social activist Annie
Besant. The entire arc of his career cannot be fully understood
without reference to her extraordinary life and influence.

Annie was the first woman to defend herself before an English
court. The year was 1877, and she was twenty-nine years of age.
At issue was the right to publish a slender volume entitled *Fruits
of Philosophy*. Composed by an American physician, the book was
designed to provide the best information available on the subject
of birth control. Annie and Charles Bradlaugh, president of the
Free Thought Society, had republished the book for a general
audience in England. As soon as it was made available for sale,
British authorities seized all copies of the book and charged Annie
and Bradlaugh with the dissemination of obscenity.

The two defendants could have cut a deal with the authorities
and avoided charges by agreeing to discontinue selling *Fruits of
Philosophy*. Bradlaugh was inclined to do so, but Annie refused.
She insisted on challenging an unjust law, and she risked jail
time to argue her case in court. The trial that resulted was highly
publicized and brought her a wealth of admiration and notoriety.
She and Bradlaugh won their case only on a technicality, but their
position was widely regarded as vindicated. In the year following
the trial, *Fruits of Philosophy* sold over 100,000 copies.

For the next twenty years, Annie employed her exceptional gifts as a writer and public speaker to champion a variety of progressive causes. She won an historic victory involving the right to organize on behalf of the "Matchstick Girls," young women whose health was severely compromised by the phosphorous they were exposed to on a routine basis in the factories where they worked. She flirted with atheism and socialism, but Annie's deepest instincts were religious in nature. She rejected the Christianity of her childhood and took up the cause of Theosophy, which maintained that all the major religions point toward the same fundamental set of truths.

In 1905, Annie became president of the Theosophical Society, and under her guidance, the organization expanded to encompass many thousands of members in countries around the world. Her involvement with Theosophy coincided with a parallel expansion in her more worldly interests. She developed a consuming passion for the independence of India from British colonial rule, far in advance of her contemporaries or the prevailing political parameters of the day. So successful was her advocacy for India that in 1917 she was elected president of the Indian National Congress, an extraordinary honor for any woman, much less one from England.

In her capacity as president of the Theosophical Society, Annie began to elaborate on a theme that had not received much attention from her predecessors. She maintained that the Buddha, Jesus, and Mohammed represented successive manifestations of a World Teacher who appeared on Earth at rare intervals to guide humanity through its darkest periods. She said the time had come for another appearance of the World Teacher, and it was the mission of Theosophy to identify that individual and to facilitate his work.

Annie committed the resources of the Theosophical Society to search for the boy or youth who in his maturity would assume the mantle of the World Teacher. In this task, she was assisted by her associate, Charles Leadbeater, who was stationed at the Theosophical Society headquarters in Adyar, India, on the eastern coast of the subcontinent, just south of Madras. There, he often walked on the beach in the afternoon with a retinue of his students and co-workers.

In the spring of 1909, Krishnamurti was a fourteen-year-old boy from a Brahmin family, one of several siblings. His mother had died a few years earlier, and his father eked out a narrow living as a clerk with the Theosophical Society. The family lived in primitive quarters just outside the Theosophical compound.

Leadbeater observed Krishnamurti playing on the beach on several occasions, and he said he was impressed with the quality of the boy's aura. A skeptic might suggest it was Krishna's quiet, sensitive personality that captured Leadbeater's attention, as well as perhaps a somewhat passive attitude. In any case, Leadbeater arranged for Krishnamurti to visit with him for a more thorough assessment of the boy's qualities.

Krishna was inseparable from his younger brother, Nitya, so the two boys went together to be examined by Leadbeater. His assessment took the form of investigations into Krishna's past lives, a subject in which he was considered unusually gifted. A more decisive determination, however, occurred a few weeks later, when Annie next returned to Adyar. She concurred with Leadbeater's view that Krishnamurti possessed unusual qualities and might indeed serve as the vehicle for the next manifestation of the World Teacher. She resolved to take him under her care and to raise and educate him with all the formidable range of resources at her disposal.

For the first few years, Krishna accepted rather passively the grand expectations that were fastened upon him. He formed a deep and abiding bond with Annie, who removed him and Nitya to England. There they received first-class instruction as well as exposure to excellence in every arena of English culture and society. Krishna developed a taste for quality in clothing and in cars, and he enjoyed the humor of P. G. Wodehouse, whose satirical novels deftly exposed the vulnerabilities of the British upper crust. He acquired such skill in golf that his handicap was one under par.

In order to facilitate the emergence and the work of the World Teacher, Annie constructed an international organization, allied with the Theosophical Society, entitled the Order of the Star in the East. She appointed Krishnamurti as the head of this organization, exclusively responsible for its management and direction. At its peak, the Order of the Star numbered some 40,000 members in countries around the world.

By the time he arrived on the threshold of adulthood, Krishnamurti began to chafe under the weight of the role he was expected to assume. He found himself rather bored and dissatisfied with life and uncertain of his own sense of direction. His devotion to Annie remained undiminished, but she was advancing in years while he was just coming into his own.

This was the state of affairs at the time that Krishna and Nitya arrived in Ojai. Their purpose in coming was strictly related to Nitya's health, and neither brother could fully understand the meaning of what had occurred to Krishna a few weeks after their arrival.

Nitya interpreted what he observed in Theosophical terms. He maintained that Krishna had joined the company of the ascended Masters, an assembly of spiritual personalities residing in the astral plane. Others who have commented subsequently maintained that the experience represented the awakening of kundalini energy.

Whatever it may have actually meant, Krishnamurti insisted that the episode remain known to only a small number of those most closely involved in his life. After several decades had passed, and his work had unfolded on its own terms, he allowed the experience to become a matter of public record. Even then, however, he tended to discount its significance.

What can be said with confidence is that this episode coincided with Krishnamurti's increasing independence of mind and with his corresponding detachment from the principles of Theosophy. He began to articulate an original psychological perspective, one that focused on the factual realities of everyday life, rather than anything rooted in the activities of the ascended Masters. Theosophists held that there exists a precise path of spiritual advancement, and that progress along this path is assessed on an individual basis by the Masters. Krishnamurti's own perspective was singularly devoid of any reference to anything of this kind.

Krishnamurti's increasing independence of mind received a sharply added impetus in 1925. At that time, he journeyed from Ojai to India to attend an international conference of Theosophists. Nitya stayed behind in Ojai in good care, including the guaranteed protection of the ascended Masters. While on passage to India, the ship on which Krishnamurti sailed received a telegraphic message late one night in the middle of a storm. The fever and other symptoms of Nitya's tuberculosis had flared up unexpectedly and taken his life.

From that day forward, the course of Krishnamurti's action was probably inevitable. By 1927, anyone who listened carefully to his public talks could discern his increasing distance from all the trappings of Theosophy and the Order of the Star. The rituals, the ideology, the image of spiritual advancement along a prescribed path, all appeared to hold little meaning for him.

By 1929, the force of his own vision could no longer be contained. In that year, Krishnamurti announced to his assembled followers that he intended to dissolve the Order of the Star in the East. He did so in a memorable address in which he insisted that psychological truth and organized religion have nothing whatsoever in common.

"Truth is a pathless land," he maintained, in a metaphor selected precisely to repudiate the central Theosophical image of a spiritual path to salvation. From that day forward, he vowed, his life's work would be to promote psychological freedom. Any form of religious organization is the denial of freedom, he said, and that is why he had to dissolve the Order of the Star. He concluded his address with these words:

> For two years I have been thinking about this, slowly, carefully, patiently, and I have now decided to disband the Order, as I happen to be its Head. You can form other organisations and expect someone else. With that I am not concerned, nor with creating new cages, new decorations for those cages. My only concern is to set men absolutely, unconditionally free.

Krishnamurti speaking at Brockwood Park, 1981.

CHAPTER TWO

OBSERVATION

To Socrates is attributed the aphorism "know thyself." The core of Krishnamurti's philosophy might be summarized equally succinctly as "observe yourself." Unfolding the implications of this simple imperative, however, fills many volumes and consumed the better part of a long lifetime.

Krishnamurti's perspective, as it developed over the course of decades, recognizes a vast disparity between the outward, technological achievements of man and his inward state. Psychologically, human beings remain exactly as they have been for thousands of years: anxious, acquisitive, conflicted, and violent, and everywhere identified with a local tribe or nation at the expense of the rest of mankind. Love, compassion, joy, and beauty represent, for most of us, occasional episodes of relief from a life of struggle and sorrow.

Krishnamurti insisted that his outlook was not the result of any analytical or theoretical exercise but was the product of direct observation of psychological actualities. As such, his ideas were subject to the independent confirmation of each individual listener. His remarks were not designed to be accepted on the basis of any presumed authority, as if he were some kind of oracle, but were put before the audience for individual exploration and discovery.

If we wish to solve some problem or achieve a result in the external world, we typically form an idea or image of what we are seeking. In order to travel to another city, or build a bridge, or sharpen a knife, or solve a puzzle, we usually have in mind a picture, a blueprint, or a concept of our goal. Such an approach is perfectly reasonable and serves as a reliable guide to successful action.

And so, when we turn to inward, psychological problems, it is natural to adopt a similar strategy. If we are fearful, we may form an image of courage and attempt to achieve it. Because human beings are violent, we have created an ideal of non-violence as a goal. According to Krishnamurti, however, this apparently logical approach is in fact deeply misguided when applied to a problem or issue that originates in the mind.

If I am fearful and seek to become courageous, there already exists within me a division in consciousness. Part of the mind is afraid; another part seeks to overcome that fear. Krishnamurti maintained it is a psychological "law" that any division in consciousness must engender internal conflict. Such conflict is a waste of energy and not conducive to the result I am seeking to achieve.

At a deeper level, any psychological goal of this kind is founded upon an illusion. It assumes that my identity can be molded, manipulated, or improved according to my intention. But individual identity is not actually anything of this nature. If closely examined, what we think of as "I" is only a collection of images, memories, and associations. It is not something that can be shaped by deliberation or an act of will.

However, this does not mean that nothing can be done about the problem of fear. On the contrary, resolving fear at its root is fundamental to psychological freedom. According to Krishnamurti, fear "darkens the mind," and to penetrate its nature and learn to live without fear is essential to the cultivation of intelligence.

The sheer observation of one's actual and immediate state of mind is the catalyst for its transformation. The full, unmediated perception of fear is the solvent in which it is dissipated. Such perception is not easily achieved, however, for the mind is quick to supply judgments or justifications, reasons why the fear should or should not exist, as well as the impulse to fix it, suppress it, or overcome it. All these movements of the mind introduce distortions and prevent the act of pure perception. "Choiceless awareness," in Krishnamurti's phrase, is therefore an art in its own right, one that requires dedication, clarity, and the disciplined intention to live a different kind of life.

Fear, desire, anger, and all the sources of conflict in human relationship are grounded in a nexus of misconceptions about the structure of consciousness. Ultimately, these misconceptions are rooted in a failure to understand the nature of thought. The activities of thought are pervasive and shape perception and motivation in fundamental and far-reaching ways.

Thought is, in essence, the expression of knowledge, but knowledge is the repository of the past. Therefore, thought is not a medium that can apprehend anything new. But life is a movement, a movement in relationship, and the present moment always contains elements that are new. However valuable thought may be for many purposes, it can never fully meet the challenge of the present.

Thought is unaware of its own nature and activity. It has constructed the self, the "I," the thinker who evaluates and guides our every action. Thought has assumed to itself the role of the observer, and in that role, it dominates the whole of consciousness. In the psychological field, however—in what is perhaps Krishnamurti's most enduring and memorable insight—the observer is the observed; the thinker is the thought. The distinction between the two is an artificial division in consciousness, introduced by thought because thought does not understand itself.

No brief description of Krishnamurti's work can possibly capture the scope, the depth, and the beauty of expression of his actual teachings. This summary is merely a general orientation for those not familiar with his philosophy and cannot serve as a substitute for the direct encounter with his views.

It must also be emphasized that his teachings are not intended as an intellectual exercise or any kind of contribution to purely theoretical discourse. He is addressing the actual, concrete circumstances of each individual listener. His role is not to convince or to prove the truth of his observations, but rather to articulate them for independent corroboration by anyone who finds them of interest. The role of the listener is to explore their application in his or her daily life.

Krishnamurti maintained that his central insights lead to a revolution in the structure of consciousness. The deep realization that the observer is the observed precipitates a psychological transformation, one in which the individual becomes whole, integral, complete. This must therefore be the work of anyone who is serious about living a fully intelligent life. Such an individual is not deterred by the magnitude of the task, for it entails nothing less than seeing oneself and the world as they are. The welfare of our species hangs in the balance as well.

—⁓—

With the dissolution of the Order of the Star, large sums of money and property had to be returned to their original owners. Certain properties in Ojai and India, however, had been purchased by Annie specifically for Krishnamurti and his work, and they remained effectively under his control. Among these were Pine Cottage and the 150-acre parcel on which the Oak Grove School was built many years later.

And so the stage was set for Krishnamurti to conduct his life's work on his own terms. He proceeded to give public talks on an annual basis in America, Europe, and India, with occasional excursions to other parts of the globe. The talks were recorded by shorthand and brought out in soft-cover pamphlets under the imprint of Krishnamurti Writings, Inc., or KWINC. Over the course of decades, his philosophy underwent continuous refinement in substance and expression, but it always embodied the basic themes of self-awareness, psychological freedom, and the cultivation of intelligence.

In the decade following the dissolution of the Order of the Star, Krishnamurti gave public talks in ninety cities throughout the world. He spoke in twenty-two nations, from Scotland to Scandinavia, in India and Pakistan, Australia and New Zealand, the United States and Canada, and several countries in South America. He spoke in capital cities from Rome to Rio de Janeiro, and in the United States in New York, Chicago, Seattle, San Francisco, Oakland, Minneapolis, St. Paul, Kansas City, Cleveland,

Philadelphia, Rochester, Atlanta, Birmingham, and San Antonio, in addition to five series of talks in Ojai. Over the course of the decade, he gave some six hundred public talks in all.

The format of these talks displayed certain characteristics that remained constant throughout his career. They were absolutely bare of adornment or any other element extraneous to the delivery of his message. Krishnamurti neither wanted nor required introduction, and he visibly shrank from applause. There were no preliminaries and no admission fees, although donations to support his travel and living expenses were accepted. There was never any kind of group or organization to which one could attach oneself or belong.

Krishnamurti was always carefully dressed, but he suited his attire to the locale. If he were outdoors, he might speak while standing, whereas indoors he sat in a simple, upright chair. Once he experimented with speaking from behind a curtain, in an effort to minimize any response from the audience based upon his appearance or personality. In general, the format of the talks was designed to eliminate distractions, and in this respect, they did not vary at all.

—∿∿—

During World War II, Krishnamurti was unable to continue with his annual travels and his regular program of public talks, and he chose to remain in Ojai throughout this period. In 1939, he met author Aldous Huxley, who had relocated with his wife from England to Santa Barbara, an hour's drive from Ojai. The two men developed a close bond during the war, based upon a mutual interest in many subjects, from the global to the individual to the natural world. They often went for long walks together in the hills surrounding the Ojai Valley.

Huxley encouraged Krishnamurti to commit some of his thoughts and ideas to paper. In a pattern that he developed, with variations, for the rest of his life, Krishnamurti coupled precisely etched observations of nature with dialogues he recalled with individuals who had come to seek his counsel about problems of daily life. Huxley declared the early drafts to be "marvellous and unique," and the result was the series of three volumes, *Commentaries on Living*.

At the end of the war, Krishnamurti, Huxley, and several others inaugurated the Happy Valley School on land adjacent to the Ojai Valley purchased by Annie Besant many years earlier. Krishnamurti had already established two schools in India, and the original intention of the Happy Valley School was to promote a kind of education consonant with his philosophy; but between the intention and the implementation, a gulf arose that eventually could not be bridged. Krishnamurti's role and influence were gradually diminished, and after several years, he severed all relationship with the school. It continues today, however, as a progressive boarding school (now called the Besant Hill School) with an emphasis on the arts.

In the years that followed the war, Krishnamurti continued his annual round of public talks in Europe, India, and the United States. The success of *Commentaries on Living* led to the publication of over thirty subsequent volumes. Some of these were composed for the printed page, such as *Education and the Significance of Life*, while others consisted of edited compilations of his talks.

Krishnamurti's unwavering aim throughout his life remained exactly as he had declared it in 1929—to plant the seed of psychological freedom. He gave his attention exclusively to the dynamic principles governing the operations of thought and consciousness and to articulating his observations to a global audience. To carry out this intention, there were practical matters to take care of, including the scheduling of his talks and the management of funds donated in support of his work. But these were tasks he preferred to delegate as much as possible.

In his capacity as head of the Order of the Star, Krishnamurti had been assisted by a young man named D. Rajagopal, an Oxford-trained lawyer highly skilled in financial and administrative affairs. Rajagopal was the primary individual responsible for overseeing Krishnamurti's speaking schedule, as well as for managing a virtual empire of property and other financial assets.

After the dissolution of the Order of the Star, Rajagopal continued his alliance with Krishnamurti. In addition to handling travel arrangements, he edited the talks for print and looked after the remaining financial assets. In 1927, Rajagopal married Rosalind Williams, the young woman who had befriended Krishnamurti and Nitya when they first came to Ojai. A daughter named Radha was born to the couple in 1930. The family lived on the property in Ojai with Krishnamurti, but after Radha was born, Rajagopal preferred to spend most of his time in Los Angeles.

For thirty years, Rajagopal played the part of the loyal assistant. Right from the beginning, however, he displayed a demanding attitude and an imperious temperament. Fastidious to a fault, he expected others to be equally exacting in their interactions with the activities he oversaw. Krishnamurti himself was by no means excluded from the orbit of Rajagopal's irritable and dictatorial tendencies; to the contrary, as the years went by, he became their primary object.

Had these been his only weaknesses, Rajagopal's overall contribution to Krishnamurti's work might fairly have been regarded as positive. His deficits of temperament, however, in fact only served to mask a far more consequential set of activities. With his undeniable flair for legal and financial transactions, Rajagopal channeled sums of money donated in support of Krishnamurti's work into a maze of international accounts of which he was the proprietor. He even browbeat Krishnamurti into signing over to him the copyright to his own talks and writings, as well as into resigning from the board of directors of KWINC. Rajagopal acquired title to the very properties in Ojai purchased by Annie Besant for Krishnamurti and his work.

In the end it was he, Rajagopal, who controlled the entire enterprise, and Krishnamurti the mere functionary who played a supporting role. Krishnamurti was cognizant of the injustice that had been done, its magnitude and its effect, and he tried for eight years to be reinstated to the board of directors of KWINC. His many appeals to Rajagopal met with no success whatsoever.

By 1964, the growing rift with Rajagopal had reached the point of no return. At around that time some of the functions he had fulfilled began to be assumed by Mary Zimbalist. Mary was the widow of Sam Zimbalist, the legendary producer of *Ben-Hur* and many other acclaimed motion pictures. After her husband's death in 1958, Mary had sought out Krishnamurti for counsel and guidance, and a few years later, she assumed the role of his personal secretary. She offered him her home overlooking the ocean in Malibu to stay in when he was in California, and she became his closest friend and companion.

But Mary was not equipped to penetrate the maze of barriers Rajagopal had constructed to block Krishnamurti from access to the legal mechanisms that now controlled his life's work. This remained the state of affairs in the mid-nineteen-sixties, when Erna

Lilliefelt came upon the scene. She and her husband Theo (TAY-o) had retired to Ojai to be near the place where Krishnamurti lived and where he gave public talks on an annual basis.

Erna's personality and business skills had enabled her to advance to a high level in the corporate world, in an era when women were ordinarily excluded from such positions as a matter of course. Theo had trained and performed in Europe as a concert pianist before settling into a career as a multilingual diplomat with the United Nations. They were well suited as a couple, with highly polished manners and a deep and abiding sense of rectitude.

Upon their arrival in Ojai, Erna and Theo were astonished to learn that Krishnamurti had, in effect, been evicted from his home and barred from participation in the very organization charged with overseeing his work. Erna's sense of injustice was profoundly aroused and she set out to investigate how such an impossible state of affairs had come about.

In Erna Lilliefelt, the legal and financial wizard Rajagopal met his match. As a charitable organization registered with the state of California, KWINC had to submit regular, detailed accounts of its transactions, and the various changes of title to property were a matter of public record. Erna spent months, entirely of her own initiative, locating and examining all the relevant documents. As a result of her research, it became apparent that Rajagopal's machinations, however intricate and devious, could be undone in a court of law.

The Krishnamurti Foundation of America (KFA) was formed in 1969 with Krishnamurti, Mary Zimbalist, and Erna and Theo Lilliefelt among its founding members. The long-term purpose of the KFA was to preserve and to publish the record of Krishnamurti's work, but in the beginning, there was other work to attend to. Among the first acts of the KFA was to file suit against Rajagopal and the board of directors of KWINC for recovery of all intellectual property, real estate, and financial assets that were the fruit of Krishnamurti's endeavors.

Erna herself was not an attorney, but she guided the lawsuit every step of the way. Among other things, she enlisted the active support of the deputy attorney general of California, whose office was ultimately responsible for correcting malfeasance in charitable organizations in the state. In 1974, her efforts produced a result of immense proportions. Rather than face an actual court of law, Rajagopal finally agreed to relinquish and turn over to the KFA everything he had appropriated. It was a stellar victory and a sweet vindication of the essential correctness of the course of action Erna had set in motion.

Were it not for the labors of Erna, it is highly unlikely the Oak Grove School would ever have found the means to materialize. The very soil on which the school was built was recovered in the lawsuit, not to mention Krishnamurti's Ojai home. It would be hard to overstate the magnitude of his debt to her. However conflicted her relationship with individuals at the school may later have become, her involvement must be understood in this larger context. There is no doubt, in any case, that Krishnamurti viewed her in that light.

Mark Lee with Oak Grove students.

CAUSE AND EFFECT

I met Krishnamurti for the first time in 1975, under the broad branches of the majestic pepper tree that stood like a sentinel before his cottage. It was late one afternoon in October, a few weeks after the inauguration of the Oak Grove School. He and Mary Zimbalist had come up to Ojai from Malibu, and he had expressed an interest in meeting the school's main academic teacher.

Krishnamurti's figure was diminutive; his dress was casual but tasteful; and he took my outstretched hand in both of his. His hands were warm and dry to the touch, but so sensitive and delicate that one did not wish to grasp them too firmly. He asked if we had met before, and I said we had not, although I had put a few questions to him from the audience at his public talks in Switzerland three years earlier.

He escorted me into the cottage, and we sat down there with the director of the school, Mark Lee, and two or three others. Krishnamurti asked if we all understood what the school was for—why it had been established—and what was our mission and function there. He touched my arm repeatedly in a gesture of reassurance. His manner was warm and friendly, and he said we would meet many times in the months ahead to discuss all the issues associated with the school.

The mission of the school was, in fact, unmistakable. It had been spelled out in black and white in a statement composed by Krishnamurti and was, in any case, apparent from the whole of his philosophy. The school's aim was nothing less than to work a revolution in the consciousness of mankind—to bring about a way of life that was whole, sane, intelligent, and informed with a sense of the sacred. The central element in this intention was to "uncondition" the mind of the student, a process that entailed unconditioning the teacher as well. In this way, a new kind of mind would emerge, one that would affect the consciousness of the world.

The school operated under the auspices of the Krishnamurti Foundation of America, a private, charitable trust designed to facilitate Krishnamurti's speaking schedule and to preserve a complete and authentic record of his work. In its first year, the school had only a handful of students, ranging in age from nine to twelve. Until permanent facilities could be constructed, classes were conducted on the ten-acre property at the far eastern end of the Ojai Valley. There, set amidst orange and avocado groves, were Pine Cottage, an office building, and a large, ranch-style residential structure known as Arya Vihara, Sanskrit for "noble dwelling." By extension, the entire property was often referred to as Arya Vihara.

Mark Lee, the director of the school, had taught and served for several years as principal of the elementary section at Krishnamurti's Rishi Valley School in Andhra Pradesh, India. Warm and congenial, with an aristocratic bearing, Mark was in his late thirties and stood well over six feet tall. He was highly presentable in manners and appearance, and thoroughly devoted to Krishnamurti and the work of the school.

The summer before the school opened, I had been hired by Mark to serve as the main academic teacher. The trajectory of my career at the age of twenty-eight had been somewhat uneven, and I had doubts about my suitability for this role. I had dropped out of a Ph.D. program in political philosophy at UCLA, and my only teaching experience was as a private tutor. On the other hand, my interest in the field of psychology was deep and had been cultivated from adolescence, as well as in my undergraduate years at UC Berkeley. The study of investigators as diverse as Freud, Skinner, Piaget, Maslow, and Ouspensky had perhaps prepared me to appreciate the scope and cogency of Krishnamurti's contribution. In any case, the depth of my interest in his work was, no doubt, the greatest strength I brought to my employment.

—⁓—

Even in its embryonic stages, the school exhibited certain characteristics that were destined to endure for many years. Each morning began with an assembly attended by all the students and staff. Mark Lee or one of the members of the staff would make a short presentation of something he or she had read or realized, designed to inspire and edify young and older alike. Then there would be a moment or two of silence before classes began.

Academic subjects were taught in the morning, art and games in the afternoon. Our aim was excellence in all areas, but the students had their own agendas, which did not always coincide with ours. One young boy named Eli was bright and curious but physically as restless as a monkey; he could not be contained in a chair or even in the classroom. Eventually, he squirmed his way out of the school completely.

Lunch was a vegetarian affair, prepared on the premises for the staff. Meat was excluded from the menu as a matter of ethical principle, although students' families were not required to do likewise at home.

At the end of the day, the teachers and students gathered together for a short meeting that Mark called "wrap-up." Any unresolved issues that had arisen during the day were supposed to be addressed and settled before the students went home. But wrap-up rarely had the intended effect. The students were tired and restless and in no mood for civilized discussion. Eventually, the practice was discontinued.

The spacious lawns at Arya Vihara, the orange groves, and the family atmosphere gave the school a sense of charm and even, at times, an enchanted spirit. But I had high expectations for myself, the students, and the school, and was not easily satisfied. The management of classroom behavior is an art that every first-year teacher must master, and some never do. The challenge was exacerbated at Oak Grove by Krishnamurti's philosophy of education: he insisted that the student should feel no sense of compulsion but nevertheless should behave with awareness and consideration for others.

A few weeks after our introduction, my first private meeting with Krishnamurti occurred, this time at my initiative. I wasn't sure how to approach him and asked Mark Lee for guidance. I was told to just knock on the back door of his cottage and see if he was available. I did so late one afternoon and was greeted sweetly by Mary Zimbalist. Mary was a slender woman, middle-aged, with exquisite taste, porcelain beauty, and an acute intelligence. In response to my request, she said she would see if Krishnamurti was available. A moment later, he appeared and motioned for me to come in.

The back door of the cottage opened into the kitchen, where a small table and two chairs were situated under a window. We sat down there, and Krishnamurti waited for me to collect myself and state my business. I was too much in awe of the man and my proximity to him to speak freely, but I managed to articulate the essence of the issue that had driven me to seek him out. "What is the law in the classroom?" I inquired.

Krishnamurti's educational philosophy entailed the radical principle that reward and punishment were equally pernicious as a basis for shaping behavior or cultivating learning. Progressive schools such as Summerhill might forgo punishment as an operating procedure, but simultaneously to renounce "positive" incentives was symptomatic of the uniqueness of Krishnamurti's approach. What remained unclear to a first-year teacher was what procedures remained, after reward and punishment were abandoned, in the event that misbehavior occurred.

Krishnamurti grasped the meaning and import of my question without any further elaboration. He held his head in his hands for a moment and then began to speak. In paraphrase, he answered along these lines:

The actual misbehaviors the students may exhibit, and my particular responses to them, must not be my primary concern. By the time those behaviors take place, the battle has already been lost. What is needed is to prevent the very possibility of misbehavior before it ever occurs. This requires creating an environment, an atmosphere, that is so special, so orderly, so clearly designed to take care of the student in every way, that he or she will immediately recognize it and respond by behaving accordingly. The student's attitude will be, as the British say, that some things simply "aren't done."

To clarify the point, Krishnamurti employed the analogy of smoking cigarettes in a church. There, one often feels the presence of some sacred quality. To smoke cigarettes in that presence would be simply unthinkable. He asked if I could cultivate a similar atmosphere in the classroom.

It was certainly not clear to me that I could cultivate such an atmosphere. I re-directed the conversation back to the terms that made sense to me.

"So, there is no law in the classroom?" I asked. He seemed to shake his head to indicate, "No, there is not," although I gathered that was not really the lesson he wanted me to take away from our conversation.

―――

In late December, Krishnamurti embarked on a series of meetings with teachers and parents designed to articulate in detail the basic principles of the school. Why had it been established? What was the basic nature of the student and of society? What principles should guide educational processes and practices? These meetings occurred on a weekly basis for three months and left an indelible record of Krishnamurti's philosophy and intentions. The meetings were recorded and meticulously transcribed and represent an enduring testament to his vision for the school.

The quality of Krishnamurti's persona was somewhat different on these occasions than it had been in my previous encounters with him. These events were more public and more formal, and his attitude and manner were adjusted accordingly. The audience consisted of some thirty or forty parents, teachers, and other members of the school community. They were invited not only to listen but also to participate in a dialogue about the purposes of the school. Krishnamurti took his responsibility most seriously, and that attitude was reflected in the quality of his interaction.

He typically entered the room at the moment the meeting was scheduled to begin. He did not wear a tie, but his clothing was selected with care and good taste. He sat in a folding wooden chair with a cardigan sweater draped over his arm or arranged neatly on his lap. As he sat down, he might glance around the room and smile shyly at a few of those whom he recognized. Whoever was managing the tape recorder that day would approach him and attach a small microphone to his shirt. He would continue to sit for a minute or two, collecting himself and allowing a few latecomers to get settled, before beginning to speak.

Most of the twelve conversations that year began with Krishnamurti articulating an overview of the purpose of the school and the reason for the meeting. But soon the monologue would evolve into an active exchange with members of the audience. These exchanges were often somewhat charged and animated, as Krishnamurti sought with all his energy to convey the meaning and import of the challenge we were facing together.

During the course of these meetings, Krishnamurti presented a set of observations that represent a précis of his entire educational philosophy. Perhaps his foremost principle was that conventional education is far too narrow in its exclusive concern with the accumulation of knowledge and the cultivation of the intellect.

Such a focus, he insisted, cannot possibly prepare a student to meet the whole of life. Education should address not only the intellect but all the dimensions of the child, including physical, emotional, moral, aesthetic, and spiritual. Attention to right relationship, manners, and behavior is also essential.

School itself, he maintained, is fundamentally a place of *leisure*—not in the casual, conventional sense of a time of relaxation and entertainment but rather as freedom from occupation and pressure. Only in a state of leisure is it possible to learn—to observe, to inquire, to discover something new.

Right education will cultivate in the student a global outlook, a realization that all of humanity is linked and shares a common, basic psychological condition. The individual is not, in any deep respect, different from mankind everywhere. The school's work is not to reproduce an American mind, or a European mind, or an Indian mind, but rather a mind unconditioned by identification with any national, ethnic, or cultural group.

The role of the teacher entails unconditioning oneself as well as the student. There is no blueprint or method for this process because any prescribed method can only produce a mechanical result. What can be done is to explore the meaning of conditioning and the actual, living reality of one's own state of mind.

Conditioning is essentially the weight of tradition, the burden of past generations, the accumulated patterns of thought and judgment imposed on the individual by society. Education in the traditional sense is an agent and facilitator of the conditioning process. In a profound reversal of convention, Krishnamurti proposed instead that education become the process of unconditioning the human mind.

In one of the early meetings, I asked Krishnamurti to clarify the essential nature of conditioning. I had my question prepared in advance and waited for the appropriate moment to present it.

Krishnamurti (K): You understand: the whole [of] Western civilization, from Freud, Jung, and all the others—and also in India, which is an old tradition—has established this tradition that introspective analysis, professional analysis, is the only way. That is, examine the origin of the mischief—whether you are put on the pot rightly or wrongly as a baby—and work from there. We are asking quite a different thing: whether it is at all possible, without this self-critical or professional analysis—can the mind be unconditioned?

David Moody (DM): One of my difficulties in inquiring into this is a lack of real clarity regarding, simply, what is conditioning?

K: What is conditioning? Your mind, sir, one's mind, the human mind is the result of centuries of experience—

DM: Even that I don't follow. As I see it, my mind is the result only of my own experience, since I've been born. I don't understand what you mean by "centuries of experience."

K: Your brain, one's brain, is the result of time, isn't it?

DM: Only the time since it's been born.

K: Time in the sense of growth, accumulation, experience, knowledge, hmm? And the brain cells containing this knowledge and functioning through the response of thought in daily life.

DM: Yes.

K: These many, many years, or centuries of accumulation—passed on, generation to generation—both hereditary and social changes, economic pressures, religious beliefs, or scientific beliefs—all that is the conditioning of the brain, of a mind.

I had anticipated a response along these lines and was prepared with a follow-up question, one with a sharper focus.

DM: Is the conditioning, then, essentially belief? A set of beliefs?

K: Belief; ideal; accepting conflict as necessary—

DM: All of these being forms of belief, are they not?

K: Not only belief, but an actuality.

Evidently, Krishnamurti felt that conditioning includes beliefs but goes even deeper. Beliefs are consciously held ideas, but conditioning shapes our very perception of what is actual.

K: Suppose one is brought up as a Catholic, hmm? You have all the paraphernalia of rituals; accepting authority; accepting Jesus as the only savior, son of God; and the Virgin Mary; and ascending to heaven, physically. These are all dogmas, asserted by the church and accepted through two millennia, two thousand years, as an actuality. Right?

DM: Accepted as an actuality—which means belief.

K: They go beyond that, beyond belief—it is so. In India, there is the same old thing in a different form, which is not only a belief but, to the believer, it is an actuality.

As a student of Krishnamurti's work, I found these meetings intensely interesting. Nevertheless, they did little to allay my continuing unease about the basic principles regulating student behavior in the school. In the very first meeting, Krishnamurti described the approach to discipline developed at our sister school in Bramdean, England, the residential secondary school at Brockwood Park. There, he said, there was "literally" no authority.

At the same time, he emphasized, freedom does not entail the liberty to do whatever one likes. On the contrary, freedom is only possible if each individual behaves responsibly vis-à-vis the group. Thus, there were indeed rules at Brockwood Park—lights out at ten, for example—but these were arrived at through a process of discussion and general agreement. If a student did not abide by these rules, he or she would not be compelled to do so by a system of threats or rewards, but ultimately it might become impossible for that student to remain in the school.

To achieve a smoothly functioning school by these means required a substantial investment of time in dialogue with the students—and these were secondary students in a residential school. It was not at all clear that such an approach could be transplanted to a day school for elementary students in the United States.

There was a small chicken coop on the property at Arya Vihara that had been built many years earlier by Krishnamurti himself. Mark Lee kept a few chickens there, not only for their eggs, but also as an educational project for the students, who participated in their care and feeding. I was concerned, however, that one of our students sometimes harassed the chickens when no one was looking. I was told, for example, that he liked to hold the chickens upside down by their feet and swing them around. One afternoon, this student insisted on staying in the coop at a time when he belonged in the classroom. I ordered him to come with me back to class, but he refused.

I felt caught in an impossible situation. I had to get back to the classroom to look after the other students, but I was afraid of what would happen to the chickens if I left the boy there alone. No amount of dialogue could resolve the situation in that moment. This incident epitomized for me the inadequacy of Krishnamurti's principles regarding discipline in the school.

Had I had sufficient poise and confidence, I could have raised this issue in the weekly meetings Krishnamurti was conducting. Unfortunately, I was not able to do so in a group of that size, with many guests who were not familiar to me. In early spring, however, I succeeded in arranging a small-group discussion with Krishnamurti for the purpose of revisiting my concerns about student behavior.

Each time I encountered him, Krishnamurti revealed another facet of his personality, and on this occasion, he was at his most relaxed, engaging, and agreeable. In this meeting, he responded more sympathetically to my dilemma. Reward and punishment were still inappropriate, but he allowed a principle of "cause and effect," in which the student's action might have concrete consequences in terms of the options available to him or her in the future. Thus, the student who refused to get out of the chicken coop might lose the freedom to enter it in the future. This restriction would not be imposed as a punishment—designed to inflict pain or discomfort—but rather as a natural effect of his or her own action.

After this principle was articulated, I often watched to see which teachers grasped its spirit and understood the distinction between it and reward and punishment. Such a teacher could adapt the principle creatively to new circumstances.

In later years, the school had wooden walkways that caused a pounding noise when students ran on them. "No running on the decks" became one of the most basic—and often abused—rules in the school. When a student was caught running, a simple reprimand or reminder was usually not sufficient. A punishment, such as detention after school, would be counter-productive. The correct application of the principle of cause and effect was for the student to go back to the point where he or she had started running and return at a walking pace.

—⁓—

Dealing with student behavior was not the only issue that troubled me during the first year of the school. I was almost equally concerned with the principles governing the school administration. There were several layers of personnel involved: the teaching staff, the non-teaching staff (cook, gardener, bookkeeper, etc.), the director, and the several trustees of the Krishnamurti Foundation of America. What were their respective spheres of responsibility and authority, and how were they supposed to interact?

I sometimes felt the trustees and the director were inclined to exercise their authority without taking into account the views of the other participants in the school. Beyond my incipient sense of injustice, the sheer lack of clarity annoyed me. Nowhere was there any clear delineation of the respective functions or responsibilities of the various participants. The ambiguity of the situation was at times almost intolerable.

With a certain audacity, I took it upon myself to compose a statement articulating the roles of all those involved in the school, from students up to and including the trustees of the foundation. I presented this document to Krishnamurti and a few other members of the school and foundation at a meeting in the spring of the school year. The meeting was recorded on tape and later transcribed.

Present at this meeting were Erna and Theo Lilliefelt, the two most active members of the Krishnamurti Foundation of America. Erna served as secretary of the foundation, the primary officer in charge of all legal and financial matters, a role she inhabited with complete conviction. Her husband, Theo, a retired diplomat with the United Nations, functioned in a supportive role, assisting Erna in practical matters and reinforcing her views on policy. Always meticulously dressed, with polished manners and conservative tastes, Erna and Theo represented qualities that could not help but inspire confidence in anyone investing them with trust or responsibility.

Erna and Theo could see no need or value in my efforts to clarify the respective roles of all those involved in the school. Everything was already clear to them, and I would be better off minding my own affairs in the classroom. There seemed to be an element of hostility in their attitude, and the tension my proposal generated was palpable.

Krishnamurti took all this in and defused the tension masterfully. He sided with the Lilliefelts against the need for any formal declaration of the distribution of responsibilities. He did so, however, in a manner devoid of any attitude of conflict or resentment. As a result, I was able to hear his perspective without resistance, although I could not find it quite convincing. He likened my role to that of a younger brother, and he suggested I ought not to be too concerned with the wider sphere of responsibilities of my seniors. Since the Lilliefelts were, in fact, some thirty years older than me, it was hard to argue too much with this proposition.

As I reflected on the school year as a whole, I felt that a good deal had been accomplished. We added a few students midway through the term, and I had acquired a degree of stability in the art of classroom management. We articulated an overarching set of principles for student behavior that was consonant with the intent of the school and yet allowed the teacher to maintain order on a daily basis. And I was able at least to broach the issue of the administrative structure of the school.

In addition to these accomplishments, I felt I had forged a working relationship with Krishnamurti, one that would serve as a foundation to explore additional questions. I had observed him in a variety of moods and circumstances and felt a degree of confidence in the range of his responses. At worst, he could be very serious, even severe, in his demand that the teachers give their complete attention to the challenge at hand. At best, he was relaxed, amusing, and exuded a sense of friendship and good will.

In any case, I ended the year in a state of emotional fatigue but with every intention to continue the exploration that had brought me to Ojai. I felt tempered to a certain degree of strength. Krishnamurti would not visit the school again until the following winter, but I looked forward to continuing to cultivate a relationship with him.

I was, in short, utterly unprepared for the shock that awaited me at that time.

Krishnamurti speaking in Ojai, 1979. In the audience are
Vivienne Moody and Mark Lee.

IDENTITY

I n the summer of 1976, I married Vivienne, whom I had met five years earlier when we were both students at UCLA. I was away from Ojai for a few weeks as a result, and was not fully involved in events at the school. By the time I returned in the fall, a variety of changes had occurred. The student population had grown, and two new academic teachers had been hired. These were young men not unlike me, imbued with an interest in the teachings, but rather inexperienced in the classroom and uncertain how to implement the deep intention of the school.

I was disturbed that Mark Lee had hired these teachers without consulting me in any degree. In order to discharge my responsibility, I felt I had to be involved to some extent in every decision that affected the overall course and conduct of the school. In this regard, nothing was more important than the selection of new individuals who would share this responsibility.

I had no quarrel with the individuals Mark Lee had selected. I liked them both and felt they were reasonably qualified. But the decision-making principle was important for the present and for the future. I continued to agitate for greater clarity regarding the administrative structure of the school and the policies that governed the role of the trustees, the director, the teachers, and the non-teaching staff.

At the time, I had the idea that my expression of these concerns was restrained and reasonable. In truth, however, I was inwardly resentful, and some of that feeling must have become evident. My notes from the year include a lengthy passage designed to defend the very legitimacy of the questions I was raising. This gives some indication of the kind of resistance my inquiries had provoked.

—⁓—

Krishnamurti arrived in Ojai late one morning in February of that school year. He came directly from the airport in Los Angeles, following an overnight flight from England. He was probably somewhat exhausted.

Mark Lee had assembled all the staff under the pepper tree adjacent to his cottage to greet Krishnamurti upon his arrival. As his car drove up the long driveway and parked near the pepper tree, this group of fifteen or twenty staff members held back, restrained as if by some invisible hand. Only I, standing at the rear of the group, felt compelled to break ranks. When the car came to a stop at the top of the driveway, I wandered slowly toward it, moved by the palpable sense that someone ought to extend himself more fully to greet Krishnamurti.

As I approached, Krishnamurti opened the passenger door of the car, and I offered my hand to help him out. He rejected this gesture with a dismissive wave of his hand. I later learned that he despised any suggestion that he was not sufficiently fit to fend for himself. In any case, I did not receive the warm greeting I had perhaps anticipated.

I walked with him a dozen or so paces up to where the group was now beginning to approach us. The staff had formed itself roughly into a line, and I undertook to introduce Krishnamurti to the first person we met. The second individual, however, was a maintenance man whom the school had hired only recently, and, unaccountably, I could not recall his name. At this point, the entire episode began to feel like a fiasco, and rather than continue with my self-appointed role, I faded away into the background.

Later that day, Mark Lee called me at home and said he wanted to come over and discuss something. This was unprecedented, but I told him he was welcome. When he arrived, he proceeded to tell me about a conversation that had occurred over lunch with Krishnamurti and the trustees.

Sometime during the course of the meal, Krishnamurti had turned to Mark and asked, "Why is Moody still here?" Mark provided no context, no series of remarks leading up to Krishnamurti's question and precipitating it. It appeared to come out of nowhere, a bolt from the blue. To this day, I do not know whether the incident actually occurred in that manner, or whether the question was prompted by some preliminary discussion about the school, its progress, and my role in events that year. But I took Mark's description at face value and understood it to mean Krishnamurti had introduced this question entirely of his own initiative.

Taken in that light, Krishnamurti's question seemed to indicate he had some grave concern about my suitability for the school for reasons based entirely upon his own observations. And that may have been the case. It was never made clear, however, what those observations could have been. I had been a member in good standing of the school community at the time of Krishnamurti's departure the previous May. The only additional observation of me he had had since then was the awkward episode of my greeting him that morning. Could that somehow have precipitated this sudden negative assessment of my place in the school?

In any event, Mark Lee did not suggest that he was caught off guard or surprised by Krishnamurti's question. He evidently accepted it and rose to my defense. He said he told Krishnamurti that I was a good and serious teacher, dedicated to the work of the school, and had the potential to make a worthwhile contribution. As he described it, Mark won a reprieve for me by throwing the weight of his support into my corner.

There was a caveat to his support, however, one that threw an oblique light on the context that may have precipitated Krishnamurti's question. Mark maintained that, in order for me to play a more constructive role in the school, my concerns about the administrative structure had to be resolved. He proposed a series of meetings for this purpose. If these meetings could result in putting to rest my sense of grievance, I would be considered sufficiently rehabilitated to continue at the school.

I experienced this whole turn of events with a degree of shock that would be difficult to overstate. I must have turned white when Mark Lee first told me what Krishnamurti had said. The sudden turn of fortune, from senior member of the teaching staff to virtual reprobate with one foot out the door, cast a deep shadow over my commitment to the enterprise.

I had no choice but to acquiesce to Mark's proposal, however distasteful it may have been. He and I were to meet on a weekly basis with Fritz Wilhelm, the German professor of physics who had just been appointed director of the newly formed Adult Educational Center. I had little confidence in Fritz's ability to serve as a mediator, but the meetings turned out to be civil in tone, and after several weeks, a kind of truce was declared. Mark and I came to a certain level of agreement, and the ongoing controversy over school structure was brought, for the time being, to a close.

Notwithstanding whatever understanding had been achieved, it was clear to me now that I was perceived by the trustees as a troublemaker. If any further issues arose among the staff about decision-making processes at the school, I was sure that the blame for the discontent would be laid at my door. And I considered it rather likely that such issues were going to arise.

I did not want to leave entirely, but I began to feel the need to take a break from the school. I conceived the idea of applying to graduate school in the field of education to gain a wider perspective on the curriculum and other issues that vexed Oak Grove. I asked Mark Lee for a leave of absence, an assurance that my job would still be available after a year away. He agreed to my request, and I set about making my application to UCLA.

In the meantime, it would still be necessary to remain involved in the school throughout its third year. By this time, the school had outgrown its temporary facilities at Arya Vihara and made the transition to its permanent location on 150 undeveloped acres in the heart of the Ojai Valley. Annie Besant had purchased these gently rolling, oak-studded hills and meadows for Krishnamurti's work half a century earlier, so the transition to that locale represented the fulfillment of a deep and enduring intention. To be sure, the land had not gone entirely unused in all that time; Krishnamurti had given public talks there on an annual basis throughout most of that period. His participation had served to prepare the soil, in a sense, for the educational enterprise that was now about to take root.

A team of architects was hired to construct school buildings that would harmonize with the land and have a timeless quality. Krishnamurti consulted directly with the architects to convey the vision he had in mind. At the time we made the transition, a single, multi-purpose building had been constructed, designed to accommodate, on a temporary basis, most of the young school's needs. The building consisted of one large, open space punctuated by three massive wood pillars supporting a high, curved ceiling with a large skylight in its center. The building was roughly pentagonal in shape, with a series of French doors at one end opening onto a spacious wooden deck. Its roof was covered in a wavy, undulating pattern of tiles designed to suggest a certain storybook quality. Mark Lee named this building the Pavilion, and it served to give the school a foothold in a vast and otherwise untamed territory.

We had close to forty students at the time, divided into four groups. The youngest students were housed in a trailer brought onto the property for that purpose, while the other three groups each occupied a corner of the Pavilion. Although the room was large and we used dividers for visual privacy and to break up the sound somewhat, it was nevertheless often too noisy.

My group consisted of the school's oldest students, twelve and thirteen years old, and to escape the noise of the Pavilion we often set up class out of doors with a couple of picnic tables and benches and a portable chalkboard. There, we diagrammed sentences, explored algebraic equations, and wrote short essays on all manner of subjects. Some of our students were intellectually precocious while others struggled in basic subjects, and even though the group was small, it was a challenge to keep them fully engaged on a common assignment. My problems with classroom management, however, were thankfully in the past, and I was happy to give my full attention to issues of curriculum and instruction.

In the third year of the school, I benefitted for the first time from the presence of a highly accomplished fellow teacher. Stuart Haynes had been on the faculty of a well-regarded private secondary school in Berkeley for many years, and he brought a wealth of knowledge, experience, and pedagogical intuition to our enterprise. Tall, bearded, and soft-spoken, Stuart was well trained in mathematics and the sciences. He and I co-taught a course in science for our older students, although he did eighty percent of the work. In addition to his other accomplishments, he played the viola with skill and sensitivity, despite the fact that he was missing a thumb as a result of a childhood accident.

Stuart realized that the wide-open spaces and uneven terrain on the new school property were ideally suited to games of capture the flag, and variations on that theme became a staple of our physical education program that year. Many students rode their bikes to school and had no proper place to park them, so Stuart and I organized a small class with the older boys and constructed a large, wooden bike rack according to a blueprint that he designed. He and I shared a sense of camaraderie that is indispensable in the creation of a joyful, vital enterprise.

A few weeks before the school year was over, Mark Lee took me aside and asked for my evaluation of the other teachers on the staff. In that conversation, I was astonished to learn that he had reservations about Stuart's suitability for the school. Evidently, Stuart had developed conflicts with a few of the parents and members of the non-teaching staff, and these were weighing on Mark Lee's mind. Although I spoke up on Stuart's behalf, I did not do so with the energy or depth of conviction that the situation warranted. This was the period of lowest ebb of my commitment to the school, and I lacked the courage to contradict the administration in any degree. I was just counting the days until my unpaid sabbatical would begin.

It was with a heavy heart that I learned Mark Lee had decided to let Stuart go. As I reflect back from a distance of decades, my failure to speak up more forcefully on Stuart's behalf ranks high on the list of things of which I am still ashamed.

—⁓—

In the fall of 1978, I enrolled in the School of Education at UCLA and embarked on a course of study designed to lead to a Ph.D. The program was not very much to my taste, but my studies acquired a momentum of their own, and the sabbatical spilled over into a second year.

During the period when I was away, the school underwent a quantum leap in its overall growth and development. About thirty new families enrolled their children, expanding and confirming the diversity that was one of the school's hallmarks.

The variety of students was reflected, to some extent, in their names, which ranged from the ordinary to the extremes of originality. On the one hand, there were Bruce and Daniel, Hank and George; but there were also Bo and Dow, Jewels and Jupiter. We had Annie and Helene, Tina and Stephanie; but there were also Rainbow and Rowan, Camilla and Capella, Didde and Dadita, as well as Nandini, Dharini, and Rukmini. Mark and Elizabeth sat comfortably alongside Snowshadow and Moonstar. All in all, it was a good and eclectic mix.

The families were drawn not only from Ojai but from all parts of California and beyond. What they had in common was a burning desire for a new and different kind of schooling for their children, a quality education in which learning was a joy rather than a dreary routine. The intensity of their dedication was reflected in the fact that many relocated to Ojai specifically to enroll their children in Oak Grove. Since employment prospects in the valley were somewhat limited, such a move represented a great investment and sacrifice in many cases.

In order to accommodate this growth, a new classroom building was constructed, designed to harmonize with both the natural landscape and the spirit of the school. Constructed almost entirely of wood, the building was actually a series of structures connected by outdoor walkways and decks. Half a dozen classrooms, a large and generous space for arts and crafts, and a room equipped as a science lab were interlaced together among the oaks. Rather than having a foundation excavated into the earth, the building was raised slightly above ground level on wooden posts, suggesting it had grown organically out of the very soil in which it was set.

Not only did the student body and the physical structure of the school undergo an increase in richness and diversity, but the curriculum did so as well. The basic academic program remained intact, but with the advent of the science lab, we had a teacher who specialized in that subject and made good use of the equipment. Yoga, woodshop, music, drama, and French were now available for all students who wished to partake of them. The arts program included a ceramics instructor who brought in kilns, wheels, and glazes. The bowls, vases, and figurines crafted by the students were marvels of ingenuity and creativity.

One expression of the transformation the school had undergone was a production of Shakespeare's *Twelfth Night* performed by the students. A new drama teacher, Lena Frederick, educated at Harvard and in England, had the courage to envision and to engineer the staging of this play with students ranging in age from eight to fourteen. Most of the dramatic action took place on the spacious deck attached to the Pavilion, with outdoor seating on folding chairs arranged under the oaks. A festive atmosphere and high spirits were generated by the sophisticated and funny material performed by children and young teens. It brought just the right note of cheerful excellence and good taste to the whole educational enterprise.

—◈—

By this time, my star had risen somewhat in the eyes of the trustees. I was not sure what had accounted for this development, but several factors probably contributed. I had navigated the third year of the school with no discernible sign of discontent. It was generally considered that I was doing the school a service by continuing my education at UCLA. In any case, for whatever reason, I now seemed to be regarded in a more favorable light.

I took advantage of the change in atmosphere to seek out Krishnamurti for a private conversation. In his younger years, he had made it his practice to grant private interviews to whoever wished to see him, and some of these became the basis for his earliest books. He told me once that there were periods when he saw as many as seventy-five individuals in a week. But now such meetings were granted only rarely, and I was careful to take advantage of, but not to abuse, my opportunity.

My interest in Krishnamurti's work went well beyond his educational philosophy, right to the core of his teachings. There were certain issues that rarely came up in his meetings with the school staff, and I drove up to Ojai from Los Angeles one Saturday afternoon with a sequence of questions planned in advance. I recorded detailed notes of the conversation shortly after it was over.

I arrived at Krishnamurti's cottage a few minutes before four o'clock. His shoes were placed neatly on the porch just outside his front door, and I could see through the window that he was writing something at his desk. I took off my shoes and knocked on the door, and he called out for me to come in. He greeted me and gestured for me to sit on a couch at one end of the room, while he pulled up a folding canvas chair and sat opposite me. A round coffee table was between us, a chessboard inlaid in its surface.

He said he had been writing a letter—in Italian. I was surprised that he knew Italian that well, and he said, "Just barely." I asked how many languages he knew, and he counted them off—English, French, Italian, and a little bit of Spanish. I wondered if he remembered any Indian languages from his childhood, but he shook his head and said, "Not a word."

I asked if he minded if we talked seriously, and he said we could talk about whatever I liked. I began by asking how long he had been speaking before public audiences—fifty years? He covered his eyes with his hand for a moment while he calculated and answered, "More."

So then I asked whether, in all that time, anyone had really understood fully what he was trying to convey. He was not at all put off or offended by this question, and he answered, "Perhaps a few." He said he could not know for sure because there was no test for such a thing. A few people had said they understood it fully, and perhaps they had. But it clearly remained an open question.

Now the stage was set to broach the deeper purpose of my visit. In *Tradition and Revolution*, a book of dialogues with Krishnamurti conducted in India and recorded by shorthand, he said he had never had any sense of the "I," of ego or individual identity. In other words, it was not something he had to overcome; it had never existed within him right from the beginning. I asked him now to verify whether that was, in fact, the case.

He replied that it seemed to be so—he emphasized "seemed." He said he had never been greedy, never been jealous, never desired power. If he wanted something, he either got it or did not get it—either way, it did not become a problem. He couldn't rule out that he might develop a sense of "I" in the future, but he hoped that would not occur.

Well then, I replied, perhaps this is the reason his message had not been more fully understood. If he had never experienced the sense of the "I," how did he know what it looked like to those who have it? Maybe he had to see it as it appears to the rest of us in order to explain how to see through it.

Krishnamurti grasped the sense of my question and asked what the "I" looked like to me. I told him one can never see it in the present moment. We only see ourselves in retrospect, whether years or just an instant later, but always in the past. "You have said it, sir!" Krishnamurti replied, as if this were a crucial insight.

At this point, the conversation became more labored. We struggled to find metaphors to express the relationship between the man who sees the illusion of identity and the one who does not. But nothing quite suited the point I was trying to convey.

Finally, Krishnamurti focused on the crucial issue. He said the essence of the matter was whether thought can observe itself in the moment that it arises. I agreed that was the central issue and said it is the most difficult thing to do.

He immediately responded with, "No—don't say it is difficult. How do you know? If you say it is difficult, you will block yourself." He emphasized the point by stating "according to K," it is possible for thought to observe itself as it arises and as it dies away.

The conversation was coming to a close, and I gazed rather deeply into Krishnamurti's eyes. He met my gaze completely, without any undue sense of modesty or confrontation. As I looked into his eyes, I had the uncanny sense that there was no one present, no structure of identity, on the other side. Whether this was a projection or a valid intuition, I cannot say. I felt he was observing me as completely as I was observing him, and yet at the same time it was like looking through a clear window, with only open space on the other side.

David Moody and Stuart Haynes.

CHAPTER FIVE

COMMON GROUND

While I was away from the school, events unfolded at Oak Grove more or less along the lines I had anticipated, but with a vengeance. Notwithstanding the growth and positive developments, a pervasive dissatisfaction with the school administration became endemic among the teaching staff. By the spring of the school's fifth year, when Krishnamurti returned to the valley for his annual visit, the pot was boiling.

Fortunately, there was no question as to whether I could somehow be responsible for the discontent that had seized the staff. I was hardly familiar with many of the participants, and the issues that had provoked them were like a distant, muffled noise. Nevertheless, the flavor of their feeling was all too familiar. There was a prevailing impression that the management style of the director was somewhat autocratic, perhaps at times slightly manipulative or disingenuous, and, in any case, not fully consonant with the philosophy of the school.

These feelings were expressed directly to Krishnamurti in a series of meetings that were deemed too sensitive to record.

As I was still considered a member of the teaching staff, I was invited to attend these meetings and drove up to Ojai from Los Angeles for each one. The opportunity to observe Krishnamurti in action continued to be the most interesting experience life had to offer.

The meetings were held in the newly constructed residence of Mary Zimbalist, immediately adjacent and attached by a hallway to Pine Cottage. With generous spaces, floors of imported tile, high-beamed ceilings, large windows, and a massive hearth and fireplace, the residence was not only a home for Mary and Krishnamurti, supplementing the more modest quarters of Pine Cottage, but also a place where he could meet in comfort with groups as large as fifty or sixty people.

After two or three meetings, Krishnamurti succeeded in restoring a degree of calm and order to the situation. He pointed out that even the most capable administrator might get tired and make mistakes from time to time. What was important, he maintained, was to bear in mind the "common ground" on which we all stood. He employed the metaphor of the commons at a British university, the centrally located area where students of all ages and disciplines mingle together. The common ground he had in mind, however, was in the psychological field and consisted of a shared intention to cultivate a new consciousness.

The articulation of this premise served to soothe the waters for a while, but Krishnamurti wanted to preserve the understanding in some more permanent form. Since the meetings had not been taped, nor any minutes taken, it was necessary for someone to distill the central lessons and to make a written record of what had transpired. To my singular surprise, Krishnamurti turned to me to carry out this task.

The document I composed in response to Krishnamurti's request was probably not quite what he had in mind. In my view, this entire episode of unrest was of a piece with the discontent that I had experienced in earlier years. It all stemmed from a failure or refusal by the director and trustees to make clear, preferably in writing, the respective responsibilities of all the participants in the school. I took Krishnamurti's assignment as an opportunity to construct that vital, missing piece of the pedagogical puzzle.

The keynote of the document I composed consisted of the theme of the common ground. Around that theme, I constructed a kind of constitution for the school, a general statement of administrative principles and the distribution of functions among teachers, director, and trustees. I entitled this document *Responsibility and the Common Ground* and presented it to the trustees with some trepidation. I expected Erna and Theo Lilliefelt to react instinctively against any written definition of the nature or extent of the responsibility of the trustees, even a statement that said they were responsible for everything. I was banking on the prospect that what I wrote would pass muster with Krishnamurti, and that his approval would keep the Lilliefelts' objections in check. It felt like trying to thread a fine needle.

I had trouble composing a concluding sentence for the final paragraph and conceived the idea of asking Krishnamurti to contribute it. If he did, that would add his imprimatur to the document as a whole. The piece he ended up adding was unexpected but had precisely the anticipated effect.

Krishnamurti had the document read to him, slowly, in a meeting attended by the trustees, the director, and me. He listened to each sentence thoughtfully and digested it. The document was composed in what I hoped was prose of an almost biblical quality—

simple, spare, declarative statements that carried a latent gravity. Perhaps Krishnamurti was sensitive to that quality and responded to it favorably. In any case, he listened to sentence after sentence without raising any significant objections.

What interested him most was the manner in which the common ground was characterized in the opening paragraph. He noticed a crucial omission in the logic of the presentation. The document stressed that there was a common ground on which all those connected with the school were responsible to meet and from which their responsibilities flowed. It did not state precisely, however, the nature or meaning of the common ground. Krishnamurti fastened his attention on this.

"What is the common ground?" he asked, somewhat rhetorically. We all waited for him to answer. "The essence of the common ground is to bring about good human beings." And so that sentence was inserted in the heart of the opening paragraph.

As anticipated, Krishnamurti's contribution sealed the deal. The trustees put aside whatever reservations they may have harbored, and *Responsibility and the Common Ground*, somewhat to my amazement, carried the day.

As remarkable as this development was, it turned out to be secondary to even larger changes underway in the scheme of things at the school. The rebellion that had taken place all spring, with the implicit threat of mass resignations, was not entirely quelled by the series of meetings with Krishnamurti. The teachers were not going to be content without some more dramatic, structural change in the school administration. The departure of Mark Lee would have satisfied this thirst, but no one could imagine who could possibly replace him, and the trustees were not about to let him go. Some other structural remedy had to be found.

To fill this breach, Krishnamurti turned again to me. I was asked to attend a meeting of the trustees for reasons not divulged in advance. I found myself sitting next to Mark Lee on a sofa in Mary Zimbalist's spacious living room with six or eight trustees in attendance while Krishnamurti directed his attention to me. There was a proposal under consideration in which Mark and I would become partners in the directorship of the school. The precise parameters of the arrangement had not been worked out, but the general idea was that I would assume responsibility for the teachers and their work, while Mark would concern himself with enrollment, finances, and the physical development of the school.

Krishnamurti emphasized that the proposal would work only if Mark and I could function in complete cooperation, like two horses yoked together. He expressed the essence of the idea with a physical gesture. He held his hands up in front of him, palms pressed together, almost in prayer position. "The two of you must be like *this*," he said. "You follow? Can you work together like that?"

When he framed the issue in that manner, it gave me pause. My relationship with Mark was one of ambivalence. I admired his talents, his devotion to the school, and his concrete achievements. He had gotten the whole project off the ground, managing parents, teachers, students, trustees, and all the issues associated with the growth of the school. On a personal level, he was congenial but maintained a degree of reserve and dignity that commanded respect. He and I had developed over the years a reasonably warm and functional working relationship.

On the other hand, I had some deep misgivings. Mark's educational philosophy and administrative policies were often not compatible with mine. We had disagreed in the past and were likely to do so in the future. How could I say with any confidence that we could work like two horses harnessed together?

The circumstances were not conducive to airing my uncertainties. The situation called for an intuitive response, yes or no, not a shade of gray. Perhaps the fact that Mark and I were intended to work on an equal footing would shift the variables involved toward a harmonious outcome.

Of greater weight, however, in the actual judgment I made was my sense of indebtedness to Mark. Not only had he hired me, he had stood up for me when Krishnamurti had questioned my suitability for the school. Now, I felt, it was my turn to stand up for him.

And so I told Krishnamurti that Mark and I could work together in the manner he had described. It was a fateful decision with long-term consequences. With the benefit of hindsight, it is not clear that any other choice was possible. I owed it not only to Mark, I felt, but to all concerned, to give this proposal every opportunity for success.

Before the deal could be consummated, however, it had to win the approval of another constituency—the teaching staff, whose discontent had precipitated the crisis in the first place. For this purpose, there was yet another meeting, attended by thirty or forty members of the school community: teachers, non-teaching staff, trustees, and a few invited guests. With all that had transpired, I felt this would be essentially a formality. My strongest fund of support lay with the teaching staff, and I anticipated receiving their approval.

The nature of the proposal had already been circulated, but Krishnamurti described it in broad outline and invited responses from those assembled. To my dismay, his request was met with a dull and sullen silence. No one spoke up to criticize or denounce the proposal, but neither did anyone utter a word of approval.

Present in the audience that day was Karen Hesli, a young teacher who had travelled to India the previous summer to meet Krishnamurti. He had invited her to come to Ojai and explore the possibility of teaching at Oak Grove, and he turned to her now to ask her assessment of the situation. Perhaps it was her very standing as an outsider that made him feel he could count on her for an objective evaluation, but to me she seemed an odd and inappropriate source to consult.

He asked Karen directly what she thought of the proposal. It was not easy to speak out in that setting, especially for a newcomer, and after a moment's silence, she just shook her head. Krishnamurti asked her to explain what she meant, and she paused again to formulate her thought. "Too much red tape," she declared.

However disturbing Karen's comment may have been to me, it gave some kind of focus to the air of discontent and enabled a dialogue of sorts to get underway. The idea of a co-directorship may have seemed to Karen and others like an excess of bureaucracy, but the wheels had already been set in motion. So much had transpired in the preceding months that no one had the energy to question the proposal thoroughly or offer any sustained resistance to it. Notwithstanding the lack of enthusiasm among the teachers, everyone decided in the end to hope for the best and acquiesce to the new arrangement.

―⁕―

As part of my new responsibility, my wife and I were offered living quarters in the upstairs apartment at Arya Vihara. This was an ideal arrangement, in my view, for it would maximize the potential for seeing Krishnamurti as well as provide a place of refuge from ongoing events at the school.

On the day before Krishnamurti's departure from Ojai that spring, I learned that Erna and Theo Lilliefelt had determined that I would not be allowed to bring my two cats with me to my apartment. This decree placed me in a state of impossible conflict. One of the cats had been with me for ten years, through all kinds of mishaps and difficulties, and the bond between us was indissoluble. If I could not bring the cats to Arya Vihara, I felt I would have to refuse to live there, with consequences that were difficult to foresee but probably not favorable.

I turned at once to the court of last resort. With an unaccustomed sense of resolve, I marched up to Krishnamurti's cottage in mid-afternoon and found him there in a sunny frame of mind. He was gathering his things together as he prepared to pack for his departure. I told him what had transpired, and he immediately grasped both the humor and the gravity of the situation. "Let's go talk to Mrs. Lilliefelt," he said, without hesitation. He saw that I was reluctant, but he told me not to be nervous and said we should go at once.

It was a short walk to the offices of the KFA, and we found Erna occupied there in one of the back rooms. With a courtesy bordering on courtliness, Krishnamurti asked whether she could possibly spare a few minutes. When he addressed her in this manner, Erna's whole demeanor brightened, and she agreed to stop what she was doing and talk with us.

Erna was dressed, as usual, in a rather severe business suit; her gray hair was cut fairly short and carefully combed. We sat in folding chairs around the metallic desk in her office as the afternoon shadows lengthened into dusk. The quality of the dialogue that ensued was like a glimpse into some divine inner sanctum. Krishnamurti treated Erna with great warmth and deference, but he was there on a mission of sorts, and there was business to conduct. He stated what he understood of the situation and inquired most politely why it would not be possible for Mr. Moody to bring his cats to Arya Vihara.

Erna was clearly charmed by Krishnamurti's warmth and good will, and as a result, she herself became uncommonly charming, almost playful, in a transformation of her customary persona I had not witnessed before and did not anticipate. At the same time, she was not about to be intimidated or pushed into any easy capitulation of her position.

In that spirit, the two of them conducted a model inquiry into a practical matter. Erna was concerned that the cats would get into the downstairs living room and leave fur and odors behind, especially if they were accidentally trapped there for hours at a time. When her objections were met with facts and reason, she came up with others that had to be met in turn. And so it went, back and forth, for fifteen minutes or more. I looked on with both awe and dismay, for it appeared that Erna, notwithstanding her charming manner, was going to remain intransigent.

Finally, Krishnamurti played his trump card. Here is this man, he said, who is going to move to Ojai and devote the rest of his life to this work. Krishnamurti paused and weighed whether "the rest of his life" was quite accurate. He modified it to "ten years, at least ten years, he is going to be involved in this work, up to his eyebrows." Whatever remaining concerns Erna might have had about the cats had to be weighed against the magnitude of the investment I was about to make.

Only at this point did Erna begin to yield. A crack appeared in the structure of her argument, and Krishnamurti opened it up just wide enough for my cats to enter in. Erna didn't pretend to be pleased, but in the end, she gracefully acknowledged the weight of Krishnamurti's logic. He thanked her abundantly for her time, and we made our retreat.

And so the school year ended on a positive note. The pieces of my new life had fallen into place: co-director of the school for academic affairs, residence at Arya Vihara, and rehabilitation in the eyes of the trustees. As I surveyed the landscape that lay before me, I tried to anticipate intuitively from what quarter the most likely challenges and obstacles would arise. I felt that I could handle the work I would have at the school, notwithstanding the magnitude of the task.

My antennae told me that trouble would come from another direction. My powers of imagination could not encompass the prospect that Erna Lilliefelt would ever fully accept me as a viable partner in the school and the foundation. When and in what manner she would undermine my work I could not foresee; but that she would do so, sooner or later, was the uneasy prospect that I learned to live with, and tried to forget.

The dining table at Arya Vihara. Opposite Krishnamurti
is Pupul Jayakar. To the right of Pupul is David Moody.

CHAPTER SIX

CONVIVIALITY

The first year of the dual directorship was notable for the absence of any meaningful innovations in the development of the school. This result was the by-product of a decision Erna made before the school year began. Prior to the advent of the idea that I would serve in any kind of administrative capacity, it was assumed that I would return in a teaching capacity at the end of my sabbatical. Once Krishnamurti was safely out of town, Erna led me to understand that my appointment as co-director should not interfere with my role as a full-time teacher. Budgetary restrictions, she said, made it imperative that I assume both functions simultaneously.

With no ally available with the power to oppose her, I acquiesced in this arrangement despite its inherent absurdity. The role of homeroom teacher for a dozen pre-adolescents was in itself all consuming. In the margins of my time, I did manage to meet on an irregular basis with most of the other teachers and to serve as a counselor and confidante as needed. The deep work of the educational director, however, entailed attention to the foundations of the curriculum and instruction for the school as a whole. In my first year in that role, there was no time whatsoever for these endeavors.

I was sufficiently engaged in my administrative function, however, to acquire a concrete sense of the dimensions of the job. Among other things, it was my unavoidable responsibility to evaluate the personal and professional qualities of every present and prospective member of the teaching staff. It was imperative to conduct this task in a completely dispassionate manner, without regard to individual friendship or sense of affection. In this process, I had observed that everyone I examined had some significant flaw or weakness that affected his or her teaching performance. Invariably, it seemed these weaknesses represented blind spots, aspects of themselves that the individuals, for some reason, could not see.

Since this syndrome appeared to be universal, by inference it must apply equally to me. What were the flaws and weaknesses in my own personality structure, especially as they affected the discharge of my duties? This question nagged at me for months, and eventually I gathered the courage to present it to Krishnamurti.

We were seated together in the living room of his cottage, a clean, uncluttered space with plenty of natural light and a view of the valley. I sat on a simple sofa, separated by a coffee table from Krishnamurti, who chose a wicker chair. His manner was relaxed and attentive, and he listened patiently while I explained the context of my question. When I had finished, he chuckled slightly and told me a story.

Many years earlier, when he was living in Paris, there was a woman whom he knew rather well. She must have felt some confidence in his affection for her, as well as admiration for his acuity in his assessment of people. One day, she asked him to tell her all about herself—her strengths, her weaknesses, and any other qualities he cared to comment upon. He hesitated to grant her request and told the woman she might not like what she heard, but she insisted. And so, he told her exactly what he observed, including the fact that she was rather self-centered. When he had finished, the woman got up, left, and never spoke to him again.

Krishnamurti told me this story with wry humor but also to make a point. I assured him that I was prepared for the worst and asked him to proceed. He paused for a moment and then asked, "Sir, do you procrastinate? Do you hesitate to act?" He illustrated the question with an incident he had observed in my behavior two or three weeks earlier.

I told him I was able to act when directly challenged but was often hesitant to take the initiative in the absence of a crisis. I also explained that if I was hesitant, it was not for any lack of involvement in the issues for which I was responsible. On the contrary, my typical state of mind was one of total preoccupation, from morning until night, with the problems and complications of managing the school.

Krishnamurti accepted this diagnosis and proceeded to explore it. In a rare departure from his custom, he gave me a particular psychological assignment to pursue. He suggested that I ask myself, very deeply, "Why am I preoccupied all the time?" But he cautioned me specifically not to attempt to answer the question directly. Rather, he said, I should hold the question in my mind, watch it, and allow it to unfold. In that manner, he suggested, in due course the question would answer itself.

—⁓—

When Krishnamurti was in Ojai, from February through May of each year, it was his custom to have lunch in the long dining room of Arya Vihara, in the downstairs portion of the building where I lived upstairs with my wife. The number of invited guests varied from half a dozen to eighteen or twenty, and in the absence of special circumstances, it was understood that I was welcome to attend. This daily interlude was a pleasure as well as an honor, for it afforded the opportunity to observe and to interact with Krishnamurti without the pressure of business to conduct or the demands of psychological inquiry.

Lunch was scheduled to begin at one o'clock, but Krishnamurti usually arrived ten or fifteen minutes late. He would walk down from his cottage and enter Arya Vihara through the back kitchen door. There he would greet Michael Krohnen, the chef and unofficial master of ceremonies, and find out what was for lunch.

While final preparations were underway, the lunch guests would be gathering in the living room, usually beginning with Theo Lilliefelt, who took his place as early as 12:30. Krishnamurti might help Michael by carrying one or two dishes out to the serving room. When he had determined that everything was in order, he would walk from the kitchen area down the long dining hall to the living room and announce quietly, "Madame est servie."

A line would then form of all those present down the side of the dining room and into the serving room, where the meal was set out in buffet style. The order of individuals in the line was a matter of no small consequence. The women and any special guests were typically toward the beginning, although there was no set rule, and sometimes one of the men had to lead just to get the ball rolling. There was some reluctance on everyone's part to be first.

Jockeying for position at the end of the line was also a matter of significance. As Arya Vihara was his home, Krishnamurti felt that he should be last in line. This was a matter not only of courtesy but also because Michael might have miscalculated and not prepared enough of one dish or another. Krishnamurti would have been uncomfortable taking a serving for himself at the expense of anyone else.

I felt I should adopt a similar policy, since Arya Vihara was now my home as well. I tended to gravitate toward the end of the line, often right in front of Krishnamurti. In this regard, however, we were all trumped by Michael, who was also sensitive to the obligations and prerogatives involved. Michael insisted that he should come behind even Krishnamurti in line. This sometimes led to a little jocular jousting for position, but Michael had no doubt that he, as chef, had to be last at all times, and eventually Krishnamurti acceded to his sense of certainty.

One's place in line was a matter secondary, but not unrelated, to seating position at the table. Krishnamurti had his own preferred place, a corner position at the far end. Many of the guests would probably have liked to sit near him, but no one wanted to be seen as seeking him out or hungry for his attention. As a result, the table tended to fill up from the middle outwards, with one or two choice positions, either next to Krishnamurti or opposite him, often available to those at the end of the line. Michael invariably occupied one of these prize spots—it was his reward after toiling all morning in the kitchen—and I was often able to take another.

Krishnamurti's manner at lunch was shy and subdued. After everyone had served themselves and settled into their places, and the mixed hum of utensils and chatter had begun to fill the room, he would look up at Michael and inquire, "Well, sir? What is the news?"

Michael would be ready with a full report on the events of the day, gleaned from a survey of radio reports and newspapers, especially his favorite, the internationally minded *Christian Science Monitor*. For five or ten minutes, Michael would regale Krishnamurti with a select rendition of topics, chosen with an eye for general significance or for the light they cast on human nature or the overall state of mankind.

Krishnamurti listened most attentively and often followed up with specific questions. These could lead into open-ended conversations on subjects of every variety, with contributions from anyone at the table. The overall spirit and tone of these conversations was casual but conducted within an atmosphere of courtesy and good taste. The table was often adorned with one or two vases filled with flowers freshly cut from the garden, and the vegetarian cuisine was exquisitely prepared.

At lunch, a more personal tone prevailed in the quality of the interaction with Krishnamurti, and in that spirit, I learned to address him with the name that had attached to him from his youth, "Krishnaji." At first, it seemed rather odd to adopt this manner of speech, but after it became familiar, the soft tones and gentle respect it conveyed seemed well suited to the individual. In any case, he accepted it without comment.

After everyone had finished eating, Krishnamurti would remain seated for ten or fifteen minutes or longer, depending on the course of the conversation. Unless they had urgent business to attend to, no one else got up to leave while he remained. In these somewhat contemplative intervals, the conversation might assume a deeper tone or add a richer degree of color. The central issues of psychological inquiry were still too serious for table talk, but more peripheral psychological topics might enter in. Those present might offer views on yoga, dietary fads, or the latest guru in the public eye. Krishnaji might have some joke to tell, one often involving God, world leaders, or global events.

At times, a gentle silence would fall upon the room, and the essentially sacred quality of the atmosphere, a rare perfume of beauty, order, and conviviality, would become palpable.

When Krishnaji got up from the table, everyone else followed suit. We would each take our plates into the kitchen, rinse them off, and put them in the dishwasher. Michael was left to do the final clean up, though one or two people often stayed behind to help him wash the pots and pans and serving plates and bowls. Krishnaji would leave by the back kitchen door and walk slowly up to his cottage, and the highlight of the day was over.

———

Another benefit associated with my new living situation was the opportunity to cultivate a friendship with David Bohm. Bohm was a scientist of the highest order, a world-class physicist who made enduring contributions to the foundations of quantum theory. He had been Krishnamurti's close friend and collaborator since 1961, and the record of their dialogues fills several published volumes. Bohm was closely involved in the formation and development of Brockwood Park, our sister school in England, and he and his wife spent several weeks in Ojai each spring during the period of Krishnamurti's annual visit.

Bohm was a shy but exceptionally kind and friendly man with an inexhaustible appetite for dialogue about the nature and dynamics of consciousness. He often held evening meetings for school staff at which various topics of this kind were explored. Although he was meticulous in his thought and expression, Bohm's manner in conducting such meetings was relaxed and accessible.

Bohm's presence at Arya Vihara attracted other interesting guests as well. Among these was Rupert Sheldrake, a biologist from England, a bright new star in intellectual circles there. Sheldrake had just published *A New Science of Life*, a book whose thesis recommended a radical readjustment of Darwinian theory in order to correlate evidence drawn from embryology with field studies of animals in the wild. He had proposed the existence of a feature of the world, embedded in the fabric of reality, called "morphogenetic fields," a kind of force or energy that serves to shape the development of species in ways not imagined by conventional evolutionary theory. Sheldrake's idea was expressed in his book with a creative flair and a breadth of knowledge that made him the darling of avant-garde intellectuals, even as he was reviled by traditionalists.

Bohm was an older and far more established member of the scientific elite, but he was receptive to those who dared to challenge ingrained assumptions, as he himself had done throughout his career. Sheldrake was also akin to Bohm in the wide range of his interests, including a fascination with spiritual movements of all stripes. Much of the research for *A New Science of Life* had been conducted while he was living on a commune in India, studying conditions favorable to the development of varieties of grain crops. With so much in common, the two men were bound to cross paths and strike up a friendship.

Sheldrake's brilliance was of a kind that sparkles in a social setting as well as in the pages of a book. His presence at Krishnamurti's lunch table was unlike anything I had seen. In an offhand and effortless manner, he held everyone spellbound with hilarious and insightful stories about the popular gurus and spiritual centers he had visited. His rather cynical attitude toward the central figures at these places, coupled with an eye for detail, was well suited for this audience, and his wicked sense of humor was appreciated by all.

By the time he arrived in Ojai, I had read Sheldrake's book with considerable care. His central thesis seemed to me somewhat glib and unconvincing, despite the skill with which it was presented. Several opportunities to quiz him about it arose during the course of his visit. I seized upon these and posed a series of questions that probably reflected a closer look at his work than he was accustomed to. He took to calling me "the puncturing inquisitor," and I gathered that further questions were not really welcome.

Another notable guest was Richard Feynman, the celebrated Nobel Prize-winner in physics, who travelled up to Ojai from Cal Tech in Pasadena to visit with and pay his respects to Bohm. On one such occasion, Bohm invited Feynman to join the group at Krishnamurti's lunch table, and the invitation was accepted. The three world figures sat together at the end of the long dining room, and I felt very fortunate to have a ringside seat.

Of the three men, Feynman was the most gregarious, and he carried the conversation. He talked about his childhood and how he had acquired an interest in the natural world from an early age. He used to go on long walks with his father, he said, in which his father pointed out the intricate web of relationships in the world around them. He said with a grin that he later learned that not everything his father told him was true, but nevertheless illustrated some larger point, or encouraged him to observe and investigate.

Feynman asked me to describe the approach to education at Oak Grove. I hesitated to speak and glanced at Krishnaji to see if he wanted to field the question, but he nodded to me to proceed. I said something about educating the whole child, psychologically as well as academically. Feynman responded to this distinction and said that his life and career had been devoted to exploring the outer world, rather than the psychological issues with which Krishnamurti was concerned.

I wanted to point out that Bohm was uniquely qualified in both areas. However, I did not want to show anyone up, so I expressed it by saying that Bohm was one who "knew a little bit about both." But Feynman took my words literally and corrected me rather sternly: "I can assure you that David Bohm knows more than 'a little bit' about physics!"

—⁓—

For reasons that were never quite clear to me, Krishnamurti rarely visited the school while it was in session. It was not in his nature to impose his presence in any degree or to ask to come there if he were not invited. But if Mark Lee had invited him, he must have declined, as a rule, for reasons I can only surmise.

He did agree to meet with the students on one occasion. When the students learned he was coming, they asked to see him without any teachers present, and their request was granted. Since the teachers themselves understood all too well the difficulty of speaking freely in his presence, no one felt threatened by or uncomfortable with the students' request.

Krishnaji was entirely natural and at ease with children, and a photograph of the event shows him sitting comfortably with them on the floor in the Pavilion, smiling and relaxed and enjoying himself. It seems unlikely he tried to talk about anything too serious with the students; he probably simply allowed them to ask him questions about whatever they liked.

On one other occasion, I saw him encounter the students on a day not planned in advance. He and Mary Zimbalist were on their way to the airport at the end of his annual visit to Ojai, accompanied by Mark Lee and me, and for some reason we had to stop at the school on our way out of town. It was lunchtime at the school, and Krishnaji got out of the van in the parking lot while several children gathered around to meet him.

Once we were back on the road and headed out of town, he turned to me and asked quietly if the students were entirely clean and well dressed. I was caught off guard by the question and answered, "Of course they are." He did not reply, but I could see he was not convinced. Evidently, one or more of the students must have been a bit scruffy or untidy, and he wanted to make sure that I knew it did not go unnoticed.

I have one other mental image of Krishnamurti at the school, based not on something that actually occurred, but on something he said. He wanted to convey how he would respond if he were a teacher at the school and witnessed some students engaged in misbehavior. He asked if it would be possible simply to observe the students without saying anything to them, and with no inward movement of judgment or condemnation—and yet with a full awareness of the meaning and implications of their action. It was consistent with his philosophy that, in the psychological field, the sheer act of observation was itself the agent of transformation of the thing observed.

When he said this, I formed a vivid image of Krishnaji standing under some trees at the school, while a group of boys thirty or forty yards away are engaged in some minor mischief. They notice him watching them, perfectly still, neither tolerant of nor interfering with their action—just watching. And so they respond appropriately, without fear or resistance, but with spontaneous self-awareness, which is the essence of true discipline.

The secondary school building.

FLOWERING

There exists a model of schooling that is considered "ungraded" in the sense that students are not grouped into rigidly defined, yearlong categories for purposes of instruction. First grade, second grade, and so on are so thoroughly embedded in our educational expectations that the ungraded model represents a radical and, in some respects, unconditioned pedagogical innovation. It embodies the implicit promise that each child will proceed at his or her own pace, unimpeded by preconceived goals and limitations. For this reason, it represented a model that we aspired to at Oak Grove.

In a graded system, the only relief from the established structure occurs in those rare cases in which a child is allowed to "skip" a grade—or, more often, when a child is required to repeat a grade. The unusual honor accorded the first alternative, and the opprobrium attached to the latter, are symptomatic of the relative impermeability of the categories of the system.

The virtues of an ungraded system, however, are difficult to realize. As a practical matter, groups of students need to be assigned to the responsibility of given teachers at predictable times during the course of the school day, and the assignment of students to any given group must be coordinated with all other groups for the school as a whole to function smoothly. Thus, there almost inevitably arises a weekly schedule of classes, which itself tends to impede the free-flowing, ungraded model.

Of equal significance is the necessity for group instruction as a matter of efficiency as well as richness of instructional possibilities. And for purposes of group instruction, it is almost imperative that students be brought together according to their level of age, understanding, or development. Once that is done, the ungraded model is already somewhat eroded.

And so at Oak Grove, we held in mind the advantages of an ungraded system, while nevertheless bowing to the requirements for instructional order and predictability. The students were grouped largely by age, though the classes were named with letters, rather than numbers, and were not quite as rigid as in a conventional school. Groups A through E corresponded roughly with kindergarten through seventh grade.

These groups were assigned homerooms, and their respective homeroom teachers represented the spine of the teaching staff. The deep responsibility to meet the school's basic intention lay fundamentally with them. The other members of the teaching staff—drama, music, physical education, wood shop, and so on—were also responsible, but their duties were typically spread for short periods of time across several different groups. The homeroom teachers were responsible for overseeing the whole of each child's education and development.

The success of the school, therefore, lay largely with this core set of teachers. They were responsible not only for the academic education of the children in their group, but also for their students' behavior and manners, social development, and overall adjustment to the school. The homeroom teachers were also the primary liaisons with the students' parents, who tended to be unusually dedicated and involved in their children's education. In most cases, a parent's assessment of the school was largely a function of the perceived quality and effectiveness of the homeroom teacher.

Each of the homeroom teachers generated a distinctive atmosphere and quality of relationship in their classrooms. Most impressive in this regard was Aliana, who was responsible for the five- and six-year-old students in Group A. Aliana had soulful eyes and a rather serious demeanor, but she radiated a deep sense of care for the children in her charge. She had spent a few years at an exclusive private school in New York, mastering the art and craft of teaching, and her skill was palpable. As if by magic, the young children in her classroom behaved almost impeccably, with an atmosphere of quiet and order that could not help but foster learning.

The magnitude of the homeroom teacher's responsibility was balanced, in part, by the limits we placed on the size of the homerooms. Twelve students was considered a maximum number for most groups. The economic implications of this arrangement were the root cause of the budgetary deficit that the school incurred year after year; however, with the exception of Erna Lilliefelt, it was universally agreed that small class size was inextricably linked with the deeper purposes of the school.

—⁓—

The dual directorship entered its second year under circumstances notably different from the first. I had managed to extricate myself from the double burden of homeroom teacher and educational director and was able to focus on my management responsibilities. Office space was provided for me, as it had not been the year before, and it appeared that the two directors were at last more or less on an equal footing.

As a result, I began to produce a series of documents that were designed to "write the school," to put down on paper the basic operating principles and procedures that flowed from the overarching philosophy articulated by Krishnamurti. Among these was a short statement entitled *Discipline at Oak Grove*. In its opening paragraph, the statement described the distinction between discipline as reward and punishment and the deeper meaning of the word, which is "to learn." Within that context, there followed a brief set of rules for student behavior.

Mark Lee and I also composed occasional letters to the parents on matters of greater substance than upcoming events. Brockwood Park, our sister school in England, as well as the Krishnamurti schools in India, were for boarding students, but Oak Grove students went home to their families every day. It made little sense to cultivate a special atmosphere and quality of relationship at the school if the students went home to something entirely different. One of our letters to parents addressed the issue of students' exposure to popular media. We asked parents to bear in mind the influence of everything from R-rated films to MTV, and to consider that what one child is exposed to gets circulated through the network of his or her peers.

Despite these contributions to the development of the school, my spirit was heavy with the weight of my responsibility and with an abiding sense of psychological stalemate. However much I tried to cultivate a productive working relationship with Mark, there was between us an absence of the kind of creative spark that gives life and joy to an enterprise. His attitude was consistently cheerful and friendly, but I could not find a basis for the deeper rapport that I shared with some of the teachers.

Krishnamurti and Mary Zimbalist flew into Los Angeles from England in February, as was their custom, and Vivienne and I drove down to pick them up. Whatever Mark Lee and I had accomplished that year was far from my mind, and Krishnamurti sensed immediately that something was wrong. Even before we got in the car, while I was loading his luggage into the trunk, he touched me on the arm and asked, "Is everything all right? Are you tired?" In fact, I was afflicted with the kind of fatigue that goes right to the bone, but I may not have been entirely in touch with that fact. In any case, I told him I was fine.

Not more than a week elapsed from the time of his return until a far more serious form of accounting occurred. Mark Lee and I were summoned to a meeting of the trustees, held in the large, open space of Mary Zimbalist's living room. The tenor of the occasion was casual at first, with people moving around somewhat and light conversation among the dozen or so who were present. At some indefinable moment, however, Krishnamurti took charge. He was on his feet, pacing about, and soon I felt his attention turning toward me.

Without much in the way of preliminaries, he asked me, "Sir, why aren't you flowering?"

At first, I had no clue what he was talking about. I didn't know I was expected to "flower," nor that I was not doing so, much less the reasons why. With the benefit of hindsight, it all seems rather obvious, but at the moment, I was stunned into a not-uncharacteristic silence.

Had I understood what it was all about, I might have offered a spirited defense. I could have pointed to the documents and letters Mark and I had composed and said, "Here, here are my flowers. What makes you think I am not flowering?" But that would have been a narrow defense, and it would have missed the point. The truth is I was somewhat barren in my inner being, and, as Krishnamurti pointed out, if I myself was not flowering, how could the school be expected to do so?

Krishnamurti's question, as penetrating as it was, turned out to be only the opening chord in the development of a larger theme. Over the course of the next few weeks, it became apparent that he was contemplating a new administrative structure for the school. Brockwood Park, which he had visited just prior to coming to Ojai, had recently installed a small committee to replace the retiring director of the school. Krishnaji was intrigued with the possibility that a committee structure might alleviate some of the administrative difficulties that tended to arise in his schools. He liked the idea of a core group of committed individuals who arrived at consensus through a process of dialogue and inquiry. Among other things, such a group might obviate the tendency for a single individual to develop a sense of power or self-importance.

In any case, as the weeks went by, it became increasingly clear that Krishnamurti was intent upon implementing such a structure at Oak Grove. Over time, the question shifted from the merits of a committee structure to the consideration of individuals who could serve on it. On more than one occasion, he asked me directly, "Where is the core of your school? Whom do you have here who is really intelligent? Who is committed to work at this for the long term?"

In fact, the school was blessed at that time with a particularly good cadre of teachers. Among these were a few young men with fine intellects, a deep interest in the teachings, and highly creative personalities. They had travelled to Oak Grove from all over the country and beyond, and they represented a rich mixture of possibilities. My personal favorite among them was Sasha Ladyzhensky, an émigré from the Soviet Union, who had made his way to Oak Grove against all odds. When I met him, I hired Sasha virtually on the spot to teach math to our oldest students. Because of his kind heart and inspired intelligence, he became my closest confidante.

Another of these teachers was Booth Harris, who taught biology to our ninth-grade students. Booth possessed the kind of mind that takes a knowledgeable interest in a great variety of subjects. He had a warm and easy-going manner, one that tended to soften the rather strict and demanding standards he held for himself and for others. He was one of the few who could hold forth at Krishnamurti's lunch table without any shyness or effort to impress, and it was easy to see that Krishnaji admired his conversational skills and enjoyed his company.

As bright and gifted as these and other individuals were, I did not have sufficient confidence to bring them together into the kind of coherent force that Krishnamurti had in mind. Among other things, they were my friends, and to single them out for special attention would have violated my egalitarian ideology. Moreover, they were too young and untested, and I was not sure they had the long-term staying power required to rise to the challenge. In any case, I felt somewhat at sea in a situation where larger forces were at work than I could control. Rather than taking the bull by the horns, I acted at the margin of events and watched, waiting to see how the drama would unfold.

In the meantime, Erna was engaged in putting her own imprint on the evolving state of affairs. For months, she had been cultivating a relationship with Tom Krause and John Hidley, both parents with children enrolled in the school, and close friends and business partners as well. Dr. Krause was a psychologist with long legs, a deep voice, and a calm, reassuring manner. Dr. Hidley was a psychiatrist with a bushy beard, a diminutive physical presence, and a friendly, almost childlike persona. Together, they ran a clinic specializing in therapeutic modalities for the alleviation of chronic pain. Krause had two children enrolled in the school, and Hidley had four, so their mutual investment in it was substantial.

During the preceding year, these two men had waged a long campaign against the textbook employed by Booth Harris in the high school biology class. The text had been carefully selected by Booth to emphasize an "inquiry" approach to the subject matter, but the two parents considered it insufficiently rigorous. They held a series of meetings with Booth in which they registered their complaints and urged him to adopt a more conventional approach. Booth resisted their demands and after a while began to feel excessively badgered by them. Eventually, the tension engendered by this conflict became acute.

Erna's interest in Krause and Hidley began when they offered their services to develop some strategies for the fund-raising project that would be necessary to underwrite the construction of new buildings for the secondary section of the school. With the benefit of hindsight, it seems likely that they also shared with her their concerns about the quality of academic instruction offered at the school. If their attitude was rather skeptical, I would surmise their complaints probably found in Erna a sympathetic ear. In any case, she appeared to develop a great deal of confidence in their judgment on educational as well as financial matters.

And so, when the ongoing conversation with Krishnamurti turned from whether to have a school committee toward candidates for its membership, Erna nominated Dr. Krause; she might have submitted Hidley's name as well if the two men had not been so conspicuously a team. There were only five spots available, however, and Mark Lee and I would occupy two of these. With Krause in the third slot, and one place reserved for a teacher, only one position remained to be filled. A variety of parents were considered for this role, people with good judgment and no particular ax to grind. In a sign of the ascendancy of Krause and his faction, however, the fifth place ultimately went to Leslie Hidley, Dr. Hidley's wife.

Only at this point did I finally become alarmed at the course of events. My inclination had been to trust in Krishnamurti's judgment and to hope that the committee would serve to dissolve the stalemate of energies that prevailed between the two directors. With the appointment of Leslie Hidley to the committee, however, it appeared that a rather narrow set of interests was being served, with consequences unlikely to be favorable to the school. I thought of the individuals involved as a single entity, Krause-Hidley, and worried that their first order of business would be to engineer the dismissal of Booth Harris.

I spoke to Krishnaji privately and tried to engender in him some apprehension about the composition of the committee. Among other things, I warned that some of its members might try to get rid of Booth. He was not persuaded and seemed to think that I was capable of protecting Booth if he got into any kind of trouble.

The issue came to a head not long thereafter, when Tom Krause was appointed to membership as a trustee of the foundation. His dual position on the committee and as a trustee strongly confirmed and reinforced his base of power. I was told by a mutual friend that when Booth heard this news, he retreated to his room and would not come out for twenty-four hours. At first, he seemed to recover, but a few weeks later, he announced to me that he intended to leave the school. I refused to accept his resignation and begged him to reconsider. He said that, as a courtesy to me, he would reflect on his decision, but in the end, he affirmed that he was resolved to depart.

Even as these events had been set in motion, they were not the only issue under consideration that spring. A local architectural firm had been retained to design the new secondary building, and its overall form and concept were the subject of freewheeling debate. At one point, it was agreed that the new building would not, in fact, be designed for the developing secondary section but rather for the middle school; the secondary students would instead occupy the series of rooms already constructed and in use. Preliminary drawings along these lines were being sketched when Sasha Ladyzhensky, whose genius sometimes bordered on lunacy, got wind of these plans.

Sasha harassed me for days with his objections. His loyalties lay wholly with the secondary school, which he regarded as the vanguard of serious academic activity at Oak Grove. The existing school building was set on a raised foundation among the oaks, with several separate classrooms linked by wooden decks. It had a distinctive charm, but its tone and spirit seemed juvenile in Sasha's eyes. He felt passionately that nothing important could ever be accomplished there.

We walked together around the building late one afternoon as Sasha enumerated his objections. Centrally located in the necklace of connected rooms was a large, high-ceilinged space for art and ceramics, a place generally viewed by visitors with admiration. Sasha made me laugh when he pointed to the high, gray walls and called the room a "swimming pool." I was not easily swayed, however, as events had already been set in motion that would be very difficult to undo.

Sasha sketched for me his vision of a proper secondary school. He drew in careful detail a monolithic structure, rectangular in form, shaped like a shoebox two stories high. My first response was dismay at the deeply traditional lines, but my interest grew when Sasha explained the internal design. The entire second floor, he maintained, was to be given over to a spacious library, a place removed from the to and fro of events in the classrooms downstairs, where serious students and scholars could study and dream to their heart's content.

Something about this vision finally penetrated my resistance, and I resolved to see if anything could be done to reverse the existing plans for new construction. A meeting was scheduled for the following day to review preliminary sketches of what was intended to be a new building for the middle school, and I used the intervening hours to draw up some projections for school enrollment for the next few years. I produced an argument that if we designed a new middle school instead of a proper secondary school building, the effects on maximum possible enrollment in the coming years would be adverse. None of Sasha's concerns seemed likely to carry much weight with Erna, but school enrollment correlated directly with income and therefore was the way to appeal to her sense of priorities.

My argument was sufficiently plausible to give everyone pause, and the architects were asked just how difficult it would be to recast their sketches at this stage of the game. Such a change would not affect the location or general orientation of the building, and the finer details had not yet been conceived. If we switched gears at this point, it turned out, not much time would be lost. In the end, rather to my surprise, the trustees capitulated, and we were back on track again to build a secondary school.

There remained the issue of a library—capacious, contemplative, with a view of the surrounding countryside and distant mountain tops. Nothing in the architects' drawings suggested anything remotely of this kind. To achieve this element, there was no room to maneuver with arguments about enrollment—only an authentic, psychological explanation would suffice. For this purpose, Krishnamurti's intervention was required.

I spoke to him in the living room of his cottage adjoining Mary Zimbalist's house. Sasha had persuaded me that only if it were removed to a second floor could a library of the kind he envisioned achieve its purpose, and I tried to make this case to Krishnaji. He listened patiently but was noncommittal. He suggested we walk over to Erna's office, where any decision would ultimately be made, and talk it over with her.

The situation was not unlike the episode two years earlier, when I had sought Krishnaji's help on behalf of my cats. As before, he politely inquired of Erna if she could make time for us, but on this occasion, the spirit of élan that enveloped their previous dialogue was less in evidence. In the austere, rather cramped quarters of Erna's office, I repeated my case on behalf of the library. Krishnamurti listened closely and examined the merits of each point.

I succeeded somehow in conveying the essential quality of the place, including the necessity for a room sufficiently spacious as to enlarge the imagination, as well as one removed from the hustle and bustle of daily activity. Where he took exception was on the suggestion of a second floor. He adopted the perspective of an observer standing outside the building, looking at it from some distance away. From that point of view, the second floor was excessively prominent, an intrusion on the landscape.

We began to explore whether a library of the kind I had described could be achieved in some other fashion. He granted the point that it should be somewhat removed from the main activity of the school, and that it should be located on another level. But he proposed that merely the suggestion of another level—a few steps up or down—would be sufficient to achieve the desired effect. I yielded to this logic, and we began to examine where and how the library might be situated relative to the main part of the building.

Erna was largely an onlooker in this dialogue, and she expressed no objections to the course the conversation took. The secondary school was ultimately constructed with a spacious library situated at right angles to the main part of the building, slightly removed from it and approached by descending a long, gradual slope. The room is the jewel of the entire complex of school buildings, a lovely, generous space looking out on a quiet meadow and on the grove of trees where Krishnamurti gave his public talks.

And so, in this way, my friend Sasha contributed an enduring gift to the school and left there his indelible signature.

—⁓—

A burst of activity surrounded the final weeks (April and May, 1982) of Krishnamurti's stay in Ojai. Among other things, he was trying to finalize the composition and the mandate of the school committee during the same period he was giving his public talks. The fifth and last remaining seat on the committee was reserved for a member of the teaching staff, but it was not easy to find a candidate who was suitable to all parties. The appointment finally went to Aliana, the teacher of our youngest students, a woman with the contemplative demeanor of a nun.

Once the composition of the committee was finally determined, a couple of last-minute meetings were arranged with Krishnamurti in which he attempted to bring its function into focus. He said he wanted us to "drive" the school to meet its fundamental intention. We were supposed to form a core of unified purpose, which would then serve to unite the school. Unfortunately, the pressure of his global schedule required that he leave the country before this vision could be fully articulated, much less realized.

In the flurry of events, I overlooked a basic element in the equation that should have been explored and resolved well before Krishnamurti departed for distant shores. *Responsibility and the Common Ground*—the statement I had won at such cost and composed so carefully, outlining the respective responsibilities of all those involved in the school—would have to be revised. It may have had little meaning to anyone else, but to my way of thinking, *Responsibility and the Common Ground* was the constitution of the school. It did not need to come into play so long as everyone was playing his or her appropriate role, but if a dispute or conflict arose, its function was essential.

Before the school year was out, but after Krishnamurti had left, the school committee began to meet on a weekly basis, and I brought up the issue of revising *Responsibility and the Common Ground* to reflect the new administrative structure. Tom Krause suggested that instead of revising it, we ought to just discard it altogether. Mark Lee raised no objection and appeared to agree. I was aghast and protested that the document had been approved by the trustees and could not be abandoned without their approval. Krause said he would raise the issue at the next meeting of the trustees and see what they had to say.

With Krishnamurti and Mary Zimbalist out of town, the trustees who remained in Ojai had little moral authority in my eyes, but their legal and procedural authority remained intact. Krause reported at the next meeting of the school committee that the trustees had agreed with him—there was no further need or use for *Responsibility and the Common Ground*.

To me, this conclusion was anathema. I had visions of stormtroopers trampling upon the sacred documents of a church or a nation. The casual ease with which it was accomplished, moreover, took my breath away. The essential nature of the committee was now apparent to me.

Krishnamurti and Erna Lilliefelt at lunch at Arya Vihara.

RESIGNATION

Among the cardinal principles of Krishnamurti's philosophy of education is that the comparison of one child with another is inimical to the cultivation of intelligence. Comparison leads the child to see him or herself not as he or she actually is but rather with reference to an external standard. Such a process entails a kind of denial of the child. It implies that we have formed a fixed image of him, which denies his living, growing actuality. In Krishnamurti's view, the entire process of forming images of ourselves and others represents a central source of conflict and confusion.

The grading of student performance with the letters "A," "B," "C," and so on, serves to weave the process of comparison into the very fabric of the educational system. As a result, we strictly avoided letter grades at Oak Grove. We found other ways and means of assessing progress and providing feedback to students and parents about performance on tests, projects, and the semester as a whole.

At the middle and end of each year, the teachers composed student reports for the parents describing their child's academic, social, and behavioral development. The twice-yearly production of these reports represented a substantial investment of time and energy and reflected a certain depth of commitment to our work. As educational director, I took pains to review and edit all the student reports for tone and substance.

With the advent of the school committee, the calculus involved in assessing student performance underwent an abrupt change of course. Dr. Krause and Mrs. Hidley focused their attention on the secondary students and argued that our written reports were no longer sufficient. They said the reports were too vague and did not give an accurate picture of the student's degree of mastery of the material. Moreover, these students were going to need an established record of performance in order to seek admission to college. There was no substitute, they maintained, for a grade point average for this purpose.

Nowhere in this logic could I detect any acknowledgment of the inherent psychological costs of their proposal. I also objected to the characterization of the existing student reports as "vague." There might have been some merit in the suggestion that a grade point average would be useful in applications to colleges, but I was not prepared to concede the larger issue without a struggle.

Throughout the fall of 1982, I crossed swords with the committee over whether to institute a system of letter grades in the secondary section of the school. Mark Lee tended to side with Krause-Hidley on this issue, and so I had to contend with the three of them. Aliana had abandoned her position on the committee, and Lee Nichol, a friendly and familiar member of the teaching staff, took her place. Lee's quiet, unassuming manner served to mask a prodigious intellect and a keen insight into people and situations. Lee was rather non-committal on the issue of grades, but I didn't mind. His very presence, sympathetic and wise, was sufficient to enable me to stand my ground.

In this manner, I felt I was able to blunt or minimize the more unfortunate tendencies of the school committee. But this was not the mission that had brought me to Oak Grove, and certainly not a cause for which I was willing to devote my life. As the months dragged on from autumn into winter, a desultory pall, in my view, began to hang over the work of the school. The weekly meetings with the committee were dreary events, devoid of any sense of joy or creative purpose. My commitment to the work of the school was eroding with each passing day.

The deeper nature of what had occurred with the advent of the school committee was becoming increasingly clear. When it was proposed and formulated, the driving force behind having a committee seemed to be Krishnamurti's sense of discontent with the directors, coupled with his enthusiasm for the committee structure as an antidote to some of the autocratic tendencies that arose in the administration of his schools. But eventually, it became apparent that another force, equally if not more significant, was driving its formation. For the net effect of what had occurred was to give Erna—by way of her apparent proxy, Dr. Krause—a supervisory voice in the daily affairs of the school.

Such a development may have been driven, in part, by her attitude toward me. What I perceived as underlying hostility from the Krause-Hidley contingent might have been Erna's idea of the very remedy for what ailed the school. This fact was brought home to me rather directly one morning in an unexpected fashion.

I had gone up to the KFA offices at the east end of the valley to sort out some minor financial matter with Erna's bookkeeper. Erna took an interest in the resolution of the issue, and I was struck, as I had been many times before, by her attitude of cold impersonality. On this occasion, her demeanor was so disproportionate to the circumstances that I felt compelled to bring it to her attention. I sat down with her in her office and looked at her across her desk. "However we resolve this bookkeeping issue," I said, "why does the process have to be so unpleasant?"

One of Erna's virtues was her ability to say what was on her mind, and she did not hesitate to do so on this occasion.

"Do you want to know what's the matter with you, David Moody?" she asked emphatically. She bit off her next words one by one: "*You can't take any thing from anybody.*" She proceeded to recount an incident that had occurred two years earlier, when I had overridden her advice not to send a telegram to Mark Lee in India. She evidently regarded this as incontrovertible evidence of my inability to accept any form of guidance whatsoever.

This conversation confirmed for me the depth of Erna's antagonism as well as its resistance to resolution. And so there did not seem to be any remedy to the interlocking structure of directors, school committee, and board of trustees. In part because it served the needs of Erna, this unwieldy administrative arrangement was impenetrable, and in any case, it had been endorsed by Krishnamurti himself.

As a result, my state of mind was one of deep ambivalence. After all that had transpired, my patience with the school and my role in it had come to an end. And yet, I could not bring myself to abandon all I had worked for. Nor did I have any clear sense of what I would do instead.

When Krishnamurti arrived in Ojai that year, it was not long before I sought him out for a private interview. We ordinarily met in the small living room of his cottage, but on this occasion, he took me to the larger, less intimate space in the adjoining residence of Mary Zimbalist. She was working in the next room, and I was afraid she could hear us. I was unable to begin speaking and looked up toward the open double doors. Krishnaji caught my look and its meaning, and, with a slight show of impatience, he got up, walked the dozen paces to the doors, and closed them.

He came back and took his seat opposite me on a cushioned bench along the side of the room. As I was still hesitant, he waited quietly for me to begin. I gathered my courage and finally succeeded in telling him that I wanted to resign my position at the school.

He looked at me somewhat quizzically and inquired politely why I had reached this conclusion. I reminded him that he had asked the previous year if I were "flowering." I told him I had realized I was not and did not think I could do so in my current role. My job required me to interact with large numbers of people and left me emotionally exhausted at the end of the day. I said I was very shy and felt over exposed as educational director.

"I am a shade plant," I told him, and thrived in conditions where I could be somewhat anonymous.

Krishnaji did not question whether my stated concern was the real or primary issue. He accepted it at face value and addressed it directly. He said he, too, was rather shy, but that shyness was a tendency one could overcome. Dorothy Simmons, the former director of Brockwood Park, was also very shy, he said, but she overcame it in order to carry out her work.

I was not convinced.

"What do you want to do instead?" he asked.

I said I wanted to write.

"Write in the morning," he said, "before you go to the school. Get up at five in the morning to write, or four in the morning."

I was equally dubious about this proposal, but I agreed to consider his suggestions and brought the conversation to a close.

It seems rather odd, in retrospect, that I did not seize the opportunity to speak frankly about my misgivings regarding the committee and the administration of the school. I had no fear of confiding in Krishnamurti. That I did not do so is a testament to the magnitude of the forces that had gained the ascendancy. The collective weight of Erna and Theo Lilliefelt, Krause-Hidley, and Mark Lee must have felt immovable to me. The real resignation, therefore, was one of the spirit, a resignation that had little to do with whether or not I remained ostensibly at my post.

—⁓—

A few weeks later, I came back for a second effort to extricate myself from my position. I told Krishnaji I had considered what he said, but I was not comfortable in my role in the school. I repeated my conclusion that I wanted to resign.

"But what about the future," he asked, "after I am gone? You have to look after the foundation"—then he corrected himself—"look after the school."

This was not an argument I had anticipated, nor one I was able to refute. If he really envisioned me in the light of carrying on his work when he was gone, I would find it very difficult to say "no."

Then he shifted gears in a way that took me by surprise again. "Would you like to travel with me?" he asked.

It took me a moment to gather the implications of this question. Evidently, he was envisioning a way to extract me from my role in the school and yet keep me involved in his work. It was a singular honor to be asked, but I failed to grasp the golden ring while it was extended.

"What would I do?" I asked. The answer should have been obvious. I would have visited the various schools and foundations with him, met all the key individuals, and participated in the group dialogues he held. In addition, I would have time for my own reflections and creative work. It was an opportunity too good to pass up. But I was too tied to the comforts and familiarity of home to appreciate fully what I was being offered.

My hesitation was itself sufficient to answer his question. Even before the conversation was finished, he began to qualify the offer. A few days later, he said he had talked it over with one or two trustees, and they had agreed I should stay in Ojai and continue my present work.

I weighed the import of these conversations throughout the spring. Despite my misgivings about the administration, the school itself was thriving in many respects. Students, teachers, and parents combined to generate a fertile mix of unfolding potentiality. The underlying intention of the school remained real and vital, and far removed from anything I was likely to find in any other form of employment.

The opportunity to continue to interact with Krishnamurti, moreover, was a drawing card without parallel. Whether these encounters were in private conversations, over the lunch table, or in formal meetings with teachers was a secondary matter. All opportunities to observe the man in action were a source of endless interest.

March and April of 1983 were exceptional for the number of talks Krishnamurti scheduled with the teaching staff. He conducted nineteen dialogues in all, on topics of every variety. This was the best possible antidote for what was ailing me as I reflected on my future course of action.

In the first year of the school, Krishnaji typically opened each dialogue with teachers and parents with an extemporaneous statement about the school and its educational philosophy. By now, however, many of those present had been attending for several years, so he began simply by asking for someone to "get the ball rolling." I was careful to allow an interval for someone else to come in with a question if he or she so desired, but rarely did anyone have the courage or initiative to do so. As a result, I usually came prepared with a question, while fully aware that I was only initiating a process that might well take another direction altogether.

Krishnamurti's general approach was to inquire by closely examining the question itself and allowing its meaning and implications to unfold. The process was conversational and open-ended and represented a kind of model or demonstration of intelligence in action.

The nineteen conversations conducted that year were extraordinary for their scope, depth, and quality of subtle insight. Each dialogue lasted an hour and a half or two hours, and the transcripts of all of them consume the better part of a thousand pages. The topics covered were focused at times directly on the work of the school, such as the nature of learning or responsibility, and in other cases, covered a wider field. Collectively, the dialogues comprise a mountain range of exploration of educational and psychological issues, and no summary can do them justice. The excerpts that follow represent merely a slender sample from a vast territory.

In the first dialogue of the year, Krishnamurti took up a question introduced by Mark Lee. I have lightly edited and condensed the following excerpts from the verbatim transcripts of the meetings.

March 5, 1983

Mark Lee (ML): We've been talking over lunch, and last weekend when we had the committee meeting, about the energy that's required to really make this a unique school. And it seems that we have all the prerequisites. We don't have any of the traditional structures. We don't have what the Catholic Church has; we don't have sanctions; we don't have all of the goads, all of the rewards that go with that. We don't have a driving force at the head of it that keeps the thing moving in a traditional way. Where does the energy come from that will ignite this school?

Krishnamurti (K): Where do we get the energy, the passion to create a school which is totally different from any other school in the world? Not a cantankerous, outrageous school, but rather a school that is both academically excellent and has something else which other schools don't have. Ordinary schools right throughout this country and in Europe and even in India are preparing students to pass examinations, get a job. That's their main purpose. To make money, to be excellent in science, or chemistry, or philosophy, or psychology, and so on. Let's take that for granted this school does that.

If it does that, is that enough? Or, there must be something more to this school, much more? And what is the more—a school that will have a reputation not only academically but have tremendous global significance? So that when these students leave your school, then they will encompass the world, embrace the world. Not just a profession, their job, their family and so on, but the whole humanity.

Here you have got a school, a beautiful place, good buildings, and the environment is quite beautiful. You have got all the necessary things for a school; you could improve it, and so on. But if one doesn't have this passion to bring about something totally new—not an idealistic new; an idealistic new is never new. Right? Would we agree that's right? The idealistic new is never new. Would you discuss with me? Why it is not new?

So how is it brought about? What will give you passion to create an exceptional school? That's Mark Lee's question. You are concerned with the school. Do you really see the ideal will not bring about an exceptional school, but such a school is born out of something totally different, which is passion, drive, and a global comprehension of human existence? From this intellectual observation, how do you bring about passion?

Later in the dialogue, after contributions from several of the teachers, Krishnamurti suggested a way to answer the question.

K: I want to find out, learn about myself. I'm not going to an expert, because they're already conditioned. I want to learn about myself, which is the whole structure of myself—not biologically, but inwardly, psychologically. What am I? I want to learn; I want to find out. And the desire, the urge to find out, is bringing passion.

A few weeks later, after several additional dialogues, I found an opportunity to pose a different kind of question, and Krishnamurti took it in a direction of special interest to me.

April 22, 1983

K: Do we start, sir? Is everybody here?
      What shall we discuss?

David Moody (DM): Krishnaji, it might be interesting to put this question, sir, which is: What would you do if you were in our shoes?

K: Ah-ha. What would I do if I were in your shoes?

DM: Yes, sir. You understand the situation?

K: Yes, yes. With regard to what?

DM: With regard to the whole of life. With regard to the whole of one's conditioning, the whole trap that we all seem to be in. Many of us in this room have listened intently for many years to someone who says there's a way out of this trap. And yet, as much as we listen, and whatever we do, we remain in the trap. How does one respond to that? What does one do in the face of that?

K: Sir, why do you put me in that position? What made you put that question?

DM: The fact that, it seems that we have all listened, and listened, and listened, and the impact does not seem to be great or profound. And perhaps you have a kind of clarity, so that if you put yourself fully in our position, could begin to see a way out.

K: Would you answer that question, sir? [Laughter.] The two of you? [Here, Krishnamurti was probably addressing "the two doctors," as he referred to them, Hidley and Krause.]

I know what I would do, sir. I'm not being presumptuous or impudent. I would pursue every thought. Be aware of every thought. I'd begin, you follow? That's what I would do. I wouldn't let—

Lena Frederick: Sir? Can you clarify something? About pursuing every thought, what you mean by pursuing every—

K: I know. I'll tell you in a minute, I'll tell you. I wouldn't let one thought go by. I would be aware of it. I would be aware of the thought, the cause of the thought, and the root of that thought. The cause may be that you said something to me and brought out a sense of sorrow. And I would pursue that. I would cry, but I would go into it. I would go step by step into it. Right?

DM: Which means watching.

K: Watching. Not correcting, just watching the whole thing happening. I would begin with that.

DM: I can watch my actions; I can watch the words that I speak; I can watch my feeling of sorrow. But the thought which is tied up in that, or precedes it, is much more—

K: Subtle.

DM: Elusive.

K: So I would wait there and find out why it is elusive. You understand—that's why I wouldn't let a thing go by. I do this all day, here. I would watch every thought, hmm?

DM: But the very watching is the elusive part.

K: No. Why do you make it elusive?

DM: I don't know, it's—

K: No, why do you say that? Is it? Is it actually elusive?

DM: Personally, having attempted it, it's difficult to see the thought as it arises. One may see it a moment later—

K: Do you know the implications of that? Don't make it difficult; that's what I object to.

DM: I'm just reporting what I, what has been—

K: Yes, but don't make it a difficulty. Don't make it into a problem. Here it is. You say something to me, and I am watching. And a thought arises—I don't like it, suppose. And then I would pursue why I don't like it. I want to know everything that is happening, inside me—whether it is action, reaction; whether it is waiting for a reward or punishment. You follow? It's like watching a pool—your reflections are on it.

DM: Yes, sir. That pool may be muddied.

K: No, no. I would clear it. By watching, I am going to clear it.

[Pause.]

DM: I wonder if there is not some fundamental, intrinsic difficulty, something about this which escapes us. The thought itself doesn't want to be observed. Or it's not that it doesn't want to be, but—

K: No, you're asking a question, sir, which is, can thought observe itself?

DM: Yes, sir.

K: That's the question you're asking, isn't it?

DM: Yes, sir.

K: Right? Answer it, sir. Can fear, anxiety, watch itself? Right? It's the same thing.

DM: It doesn't seem like the same thing. The fear, the anxiety, which is an emotion—the *feeling*—one can observe.

K: No—no—can that feeling *watch itself?* Not, [I am] watching the feeling. You understand?

DM: Mm-hmm.

K: Can that thinking be conscious of itself? Am I putting—you understand what my question is?

DM: Yes, sir!

K: Go into it, sir, step by step. I see, for example, institutions, organizations, have not changed man. I have examined the institutions all over the world for the purpose of changing man and making him better.

Institution is, say, going to the priest. I am suffering, I go to him, and he gives me some palliative. Some kind of silly, comforting words. I leave him, but the suffering is there when I get home. Right? So, I realize, thought realizes—*thought realizes, thought itself realizes*—it has not been helped.

DM: Mm-hmm.

K: Are you quite sure of this?

DM: I think so.

[Laughter.]

K: No, no, no, no, no—don't play with words. Thought created the priest, the organization; and thought went to it and said, "Please help me." Hmm? When it gets home, it's there—suffering.

DM: Mm-hmm.

K: So thought *itself* realizes that it—

DM: —that it has not been helped.

K: —not been helped.

DM: Yes, sir.

K: *So thought is aware of its own activity.* You're getting it, what I'm talking about? So, thought is realizing its own activity. Right?

DM: Yes.

K: So, *thought is aware of itself*!

So, I've learned something tremendously important. Thought, which is consciousness, can become aware of itself. Not, I am aware of thinking. That's a tremendous discovery, isn't it?

Sir, do you realize very few people have realized this? That thought can be aware of itself? Thinking can be aware of its own thinking. And therefore, consciousness, which is the movement of thought, can be aware of itself. That's all I've said. If thought realizes this fact, something tremendously important has taken place—like a blind man suddenly seeing the blue sky. Naturally, sir—you understand?

In one of the last dialogues of the year, Krishnamurti began with a lyrical description of the essential nature of friendship.

May 5, 1983

K: What shall we talk about?

[Pause.]

K: Nobody has anything to discuss?

DM: Maybe it would be interesting to go over again something you said in San Francisco about two friends walking and talking.

K: Shall we talk about that?
          Suppose Dr. Krause and I are friends—I hope we are—what would I expect of him, or what would he expect of me? Or, he doesn't expect anything from me, or I from him. He's a friend.
          I like to discuss with him about everything—about myself, and, if he is willing, he would discuss about himself with me. There'd be a certain mutual respect. I won't take anything for granted and he won't, either. I would expect him to see what my difficulty is, as he would expect me to look at his difficulties. It'd be a mutual interaction of communication without any barrier, without any kind of resistance. He won't try to dominate me, or I him. We'd go along talking about various things. If it happens to be in a lane crowded with trees and birds, we'd sit down and talk.
          I would call that friendship: easy communication, not merely verbally but a communication of affection, friendship. We'd be very careful not to tread on each other's toes, but we are willing to tread on our toes. Would you call that friendship?

Because I don't mind exposing myself to him, he would understand. I would say my problems, that I smoke, drink, whatever it is. But also, if I am inclined, if both of us are serious, we'd probe into something much more difficult. If we were mutually interested, we would carry on a conversation about the universe, or why I cannot get on well with my wife or with my husband. I would discuss *everything* without any restraint, right, sir? Would you call that friendship?

And are we friends like that? Not only Dr. Krause and I, but the rest of us? I've only known him two years, isn't it, sir? Some of you I've known perhaps twenty or forty years or more. Are we such friends? If not, why?

I would like to have a conversation with him, with my friend—a conversation about why America is becoming what it is: eccentric, experimenting with one thing after another endlessly—right?—and so on. I'd like to discuss, talk it over.

Now, can we discuss like that, you and I, without *any* restraint, unashamed, direct, clear? Could we do that? Can we communicate with each other? Come on, sirs.

LF: Sir, I think we *are* restrained, and we *are* ashamed, and we *do* hide.

K: Why? We are friends.

LF: I know.

K: What are you ashamed about?

LF: I don't know. I mean perhaps because we don't go deeply enough, so we just…

K: No, no, I don't think it's a question—if I may contradict you—friendship admits that. I'm ashamed, but I don't mind talking about it. I don't mind talking about anything about myself. I don't mind saying, "Look, I've done something rather ugly a few years ago. I'm sorry it has happened, but there it is." You follow?

Not that I want to talk to everybody in the bus. [Laughter.]
I won't. I was standing once in some station in America—I've
forgotten where, Chicago—taking a train, and a total stranger
comes along, comes to me and puts his arm around me and says,
"Brother, what's your racket?"

[Laughter.]

That's familiarity, you follow, that's not friendship. Is it
possible to be friendly without familiarity? Is that what you're
objecting to, that friendship includes familiarity?

Who is willing here—if I may ask in great friendship—who
is willing to talk with me quite openly, easily, without any af-
fectation, knowing I won't dominate, and you won't dominate?
I won't interfere, and I will see that you don't interfere, but communication. Is that impossible?

———

By the time of Krishnamurti's departure from Ojai in May, I had
agreed to stay on at the school, if only by default, since I could not
bring myself to leave. I felt the net effect of my conversations with
him was that he had asked me to stay, not only for the present but
for the distant future. Despite my misgivings, I was not prepared
to say "no" to such a request.

Nevertheless, my deep antipathy for the committee and the
course in which it was taking the school had not been addressed
or resolved. In the absence of my resignation, such an attitude had
to find some other means of expression, and it did. It came in the
last week or two of the school year, late one afternoon, in the hour
when dusk begins to gather itself and settle upon the land.

Mark Lee and I were sitting out on one of the classroom decks,
examining the anticipated enrollment figures for the coming
summer and fall. The figures were not favorable, and for the first
time in eight years, it looked as though Oak Grove's enrollment
might not increase. As the shadows lengthened across the playing

field and the meadows, I suggested to Mark there might be a meaning for us in the numbers. In principle, he and I were still in charge of the school, and we had every right to confer with one another independently of the committee. The time had come to test where his loyalties lay.

I told him I felt the projected decline in enrollment had a cause. A kind of shadow had fallen over the life of the school, I suggested. There was a cloud of malaise or discontent whose origin could be traced to the advent of the school committee. I did not suggest any particular prescription to remedy this malaise. The diagnosis had sufficient gravity in itself.

Mark Lee's response was non-committal. He neither supported nor opposed my interpretation but appeared simply to absorb it thoughtfully. Our meeting ended without much further discussion.

The next regularly scheduled meeting of the committee occurred two or three days later. In that interval, Mark Lee said nothing to me about my revelation to him, and I had begun to wonder if it had even registered. He gave no hint or clue that he had considered it—much less discussed it with other members of the committee.

Yet, when we sat down to meet—Dr. Krause, Mrs. Hidley, Lee Nichol, Mark, and I—my confidential comments turned out to be the first order of business. Before we had even settled into our chairs, Tom Krause turned to me and announced that he understood I had some major concerns about the committee and its conduct.

I was by no means prepared to confide my reservations in that setting. I did not trust Krause-Hidley and felt certain that any further airing of my attitude would only compound the problem.

Lee Nichol knew nothing of what I had said to Mark, but he was attuned to my feelings generally, and he quickly caught the nuances of the situation. I acknowledged having made a vague, offhand remark to the effect that all was not right with the life of the school, and thereafter Lee stepped in and took up arms against my adversaries. He shared his own concerns for a precious few moments while I picked myself up psychologically and gathered what remained of my wits. After that, I was able to deflect the issue, and the committee moved on to other business.

With this meeting, a kind of line had been drawn in the sand. Mark Lee had unequivocally cast his lot with Krause-Hidley and he did so in a manner that put me in an awkward position. He could easily have asked if I would mind if he shared my thoughts with the others. He could even have warned me that he felt obligated to tell them what I had said whether I liked it or not. But he took a third course—he informed them without telling me he had done so. The direction of his loyalties could not have been made more transparent.

What implications this held for the future were impossible to ascertain. I was not really angry, and I had no taste for revenge. All I wanted was to find some way to conduct myself honorably, with respect for the intent of the school, in a situation that felt increasingly conflicted and confused.

As I ruminated over the course of events during the summer months, those clouds that had gathered over the school began to turn dark and foreboding and suggested the possibility of an impending storm.

The pepper tree in front of Krishnamurti's cottage.

CHAPTER NINE

NAMES

One of the defining characteristics of the culture of the school was the quality of relationship between teachers and students. Rather than an autocratic, one-sided relationship, Krishnamurti wanted us to cultivate a spirit of freedom and two-way communication. Class size was kept small primarily for this reason, and Krishnamurti emphasized that the student should feel completely cared for and at home.

The very architecture of the school buildings reflected this theme. Teachers' living quarters were situated directly over the classrooms. Originally, the design was for upper and lower floors to be connected by an internal staircase, so that the students would be literally coming into the teachers' living area. The fire department, however, insisted on an external staircase, and this vision was never realized. But the idea that teacher and student should cultivate a close bond remained central to the work of the school.

One of the manifestations of this theme was that teachers and students were all on a first-name basis. Even the youngest students addressed their teacher by his or her first name. This policy did not seem to entail any diminished expectation for the quality of the students' behavior, nor any sense of familiarity or lack of respect. In any case, it was a convention with well-established roots, and everyone involved, including parents, seemed quite comfortable with it.

Early on in the next school year, I dropped by Mark Lee's office one morning to see what was on our agenda for the day. He was waiting to see me with a specific proposal he wished to discuss. In a recent conversation with Krause-Hidley, an idea had surfaced that met with his approval. He was eager to share it with me and find out how soon we could implement it in the school.

Mark said that for students to address teachers by their first names represented a subtle form of disrespect and contributed to an atmosphere of excessive familiarity. He wanted to know if I would agree that we should have students begin addressing their teachers as "Mr." or "Mrs." and their last names.

It took me a while to comprehend the import of this suggestion. I knew intuitively that it would represent a shift in the culture of the school, but it was hard to assess its magnitude. On the surface, it seemed to be a rather little thing, but the devil is all too often in the details. In any case, my instinct was to refer such issues to the teachers for their collective assessment, and that appeared to be the obvious course of action in this case.

When the matter came up for consideration at the next meeting of teachers and staff, it was not greeted with enthusiasm. No one could see the necessity to change the existing protocol. A few teachers pointed out the awkwardness of introducing such a change. Others suggested it was a solution in search of a problem. What state of affairs was this shift designed to address?

The unspoken hope of most of those present was that this proposal would go quietly away.

Mark Lee and the two doctors, however, had the bit between their teeth. Their ascendancy had so far occurred without leaving much imprint on the school, but now they had an issue where their influence could be felt in a pervasive manner. And if the teachers were not receptive to their proposal, there now existed other means to achieve their aims.

A fundamental feature of independent schools is the presence of a governing board, consisting typically of parents, alumni, donors, and other members of the local community. By virtue of the bylaws and founding documents of the KFA, the trustees held the responsibility for Oak Grove that a school board would hold in other schools. They were responsible to set the fundamental direction and policy of the school, to hire its director, and to look after the general welfare of the school, financially and otherwise. The KFA had other responsibilities as well, unrelated to Oak Grove, but that was no obstacle to its functioning as a school board.

Tom Krause conceived of creating a school board that would represent another layer of oversight between the school and the KFA. Such a board would consist of a subset of foundation trustees along with a small handful of parents, and it would meet for the exclusive purpose of considering school issues.

I found this proposal an exercise in absurdity. Our school of less than a hundred students was already saddled with two directors, a school committee, and the existing Foundation. To add yet another layer of oversight bordered, in my judgment, on the surreal.

Nevertheless, in Krishnamurti's absence, the trustees approved Krause's proposal early in the new school year. Among the parents appointed to the board was Dr. John Hidley, Krause's friend and business partner, whose wife already served on the school committee. With this appointment, the ascendancy of the Krause-Hidley faction achieved its apex, and a velvet revolution in the structure of the school was now complete.

In its very first meeting, the school board took up the issue of how students at the school should address their teachers. We met around the long dining table at Arya Vihara, where Krishnamurti held his lunchtime meals when he was in the valley. Present at the meeting were the two doctors, Krause and Hidley, three or four trustees of the KFA, Mark Lee, and I. The contrast with the way the issue had been viewed by the teachers could not have been sharper. I was the only one present who expressed any reservations about the proposed change in school policy.

Mark Lee and Krause-Hidley had already staked out their views on the matter, and Erna and Theo Lilliefelt fell promptly into line with them. Theo brought a European sensibility to the issue, and both he and Erna were conservative in their tastes and lifestyle. The only possible counterweight at the table was the voice of Mary Zimbalist, Krishnamurti's companion when he was not in India. But she, too, weighed in with an anecdote about a sales clerk half her age who had addressed her as "Mary," and she commented on the excessive familiarity endemic in American culture.

It fell to me to offer whatever defense I could muster of the views of the teachers. I did not really address the merits of the issue—the table was too stacked against any views contrary to those already expressed. Instead, I merely reported that the teachers did not see any need to introduce this change and argued that they deserved to have the final say in the matter. The board might wish to express its judgment but ought not to issue any edicts on a subject of this kind.

This suggestion was dismissed out of hand. When it came to a vote, the opinion of the board was unanimous, except for me. I abstained on grounds that the issue was not appropriate for the board to entertain. This outcome filled me with a sense of foreboding. I could hardly imagine reporting to the teachers what had occurred.

It would be another two months before Krishnamurti arrived on the scene, and in that interval, word of the board's action filtered into every corner of the school community. Krause-Hidley vaulted from obscurity onto center stage. The board's decision was unpalatable, in both substance and procedure, and had the effect of galvanizing not only the teachers but—of far greater weight— the larger community of parents.

The first day that Krishnamurti came to lunch at Arya Vihara that winter, he was presented with a petition signed by the majority of parents. It did not contain any specific demands but spoke in general terms about a feeling of discontent with the direction of the school and its decision-making processes.

Perhaps twenty people were present for lunch that day, including trustees, directors, and employees of the school and foundation. I was seated in my usual place near the end of the table, immediately to Krishnamurti's left. After everyone had eaten, he turned to me to explain what facts or circumstances had engendered such a sense of consternation among the parents.

If he had asked me in private to tell him what was going on, I might have said, "Sir, a small group of parents has been elevated to a position of dominance in the school, and they are beginning to throw their weight around." In a forum as public as the lunch table, I could not be so frank. I assumed he had already been informed about the issue of first and last names, but the petition spoke in broader terms, and I thought he was looking for a larger or deeper analysis. I told him there was a problem of communication among the various elements of the school—teachers, parents, and administrators.

Krishnamurti's response to my feeble analysis was scathing. "Communication?" he repeated two or three times with incredulity. He struggled to find words to express his contempt for this vague abstraction. Finally, he said, "If I were having a problem with Mrs. Zimbalist, and I told her it was a matter of 'communication,' she would throw a brick at me!"

It was beyond comprehension that the gentle and elegant Mary Zimbalist would ever under any circumstances throw a brick at anyone, much less at Krishnaji, and I could not grasp the metaphorical meaning behind this image.

Krishnamurti wanted to make sure I understood the gravity of the situation. "Listen, sir. Suppose you were told you must solve this problem immediately, today. Otherwise—what is the phrase?—*heads will roll*."

He evidently thought this would prompt me to bring the matter into focus, but it only drove me further into my shell. After lunch was finally over, one of the onlookers, a visitor from France whom I knew only slightly, offered me a hug of encouragement and support. The look on her face suggested she thought I had narrowly escaped sudden death.

But it was not for me to explain to Krishnamurti what had gone wrong in the school. For that, he had to meet with the parents and hear it directly from them. A week or two later, a meeting for this purpose was held in the Pavilion, where all the parents, teachers, and trustees could attend together. Krishnaji sat on a small, straight-backed chair in the front of the room as the unruly masses gathered to voice their discontent. His diminutive figure was composed and unafraid as he looked out over a sea of uneasy feelings.

When the meeting began, it was not really clear where Krishnamurti's sympathies lay. By this point, he had had plenty of time to be briefed regarding the circumstances that had induced so many parents to register their discontent. The prevailing view among the trustees was that the parents had been seized by a spirit of dissension, and this in itself was the problem. The trustees were certainly in no mood to reverse their decision about names. The best they could hope for in this meeting, perhaps, was that the parents would discredit themselves by raising their voices or expressing some kind of misplaced hostility.

In fact, everyone was on their best behavior. Krishnamurti began by inviting the parents to express whatever was troubling them, but no one was prepared to act as an official spokesperson. The trouble that was afoot in the school was somewhat inchoate in nature and varied in some respects from one individual to the next. As a result, the first several people who spoke did not provide much in the way of clarity, and Krishnamurti began to show signs of impatience.

After about half an hour of this, a man in one of the middle rows began to address Krishnamurti in a voice he found more comprehensible. This man had moved his wife and four children to Ojai from their home in Venezuela to enroll them in the school. He said he did not sign the petition because he felt it was not the best way for the parents to express their concerns; however, he shared many of their feelings. Then he stated what he thought was the central problem.

"There is fear in the school," said the man from Venezuela. He did not say what the source of the fear was, but the implication was clear: it lay somewhere in the convoluted administrative structure.

To me, this seemed a somewhat odd formulation of the problem, not much better than my characterization of the issue as one of "communication." But to Krishnamurti, the words of the man from Venezuela evidently sounded like a clarion bell. His attitude suddenly shifted from distracted and somewhat baffled to focused and determined.

Now he began to speak. He made it clear that an atmosphere of fear was utterly anathema to everything the school was designed to accomplish. He vowed to investigate the source of the fear and to root it out, wherever it may lie. He would go after it, he pledged, "like a terrier," until it was eradicated from the school.

It remained to be seen whether he would or could make good on this vow. To get to the bottom of fear in the school, in my view, he would have to go all the way to Erna, and that seemed rather unlikely. Almost everyone else, however, was probably fair game, and it would be interesting to see whether and how he carried out his promise and with what consequences.

In the days and weeks that followed, the method and manner of Krishnamurti's investigation were matters I was not privileged to observe. On the contrary, as one of the participants in the administrative structure under examination, I was excluded from many of the meetings and consultations. I was aware, however, that the faculty met with him on two or three occasions, and those meetings may have proven to be pivotal. Krishnamurti had an underlying sympathy with those who had chosen teaching as a vocation, even if his personal relationship with the trustees was much closer. If the parents were the sparkplugs of the engine of change, the teachers were the gasoline.

When the time came for Krishnamurti to share his findings with me, I could not exclude the possibility of any given outcome. Erna and the trustees were strongly invested in the status quo, and I did not really anticipate that any proposed resolution would be more than superficial and cosmetic. I assumed my own fate hung in the balance but had long ago made peace with the prospect of leaving the school.

I was called to meet with Krishnamurti and Mary Zimbalist in his cottage. He spoke in warm and friendly terms and confided in me his current thinking about events in the school. He and those closest to him had reached a tentative decision. They had concluded that the Krause-Hidley faction needed to be dismantled and removed from any further influence in the school. He wanted to know if I agreed with that assessment.

Needless to say, I endorsed this recommendation. Inwardly, I rejoiced, even as I could hardly believe my ears. Krishnamurti had delivered on his promise to root out the source of fear in the school to a degree I frankly had not thought possible. I still expected Erna to somehow intervene and undo the deal that seemed to be in the works. But if I could take his description of the situation at face value, deliverance was at hand.

It was not the custom of the KFA simply to dismiss its members when their participation was no longer considered helpful. In the rare cases where action was required, the member in question was given the opportunity to resign, perhaps with some encouragement. Krause and Hidley, however, were not inclined to go gently into that good night.

A meeting of the KFA was scheduled to implement their departure. The following day, I stood with Krishnaji at the rear of the lunch line and he described to me what had taken place.

The meeting was long and arduous; the two doctors stood their ground and argued against every reason given why they should resign. Dr. Krause employed a physical gesture to indicate what would happen to the school without their guidance: he held his hand out flat, palm towards the ground, and made a short, sharp downward motion.

In the end, Krause agreed that he would resign if Erna herself stated forthrightly that this was her preference. It was a fitting means of resolution, since he had been her man, in my view, from the beginning. Perhaps somewhat reluctantly, she affirmed that he and Hidley should resign from the foundation and the school board, and the meeting came to a conclusion.

With the departure of Krause and Hidley, one of the central issues vexing the school community was resolved. The storm of controversy had not yet spent its force, but for the moment, a spirit of peace prevailed. In that interval, an hour of leisure opened up one day around the lunch table. Everyone had finished eating, and Krishnaji asked what had become of the issue whose spark had ignited a conflagration. Did the students at the school still address the teachers by their first names?

The polarization that had consumed the school culture was now in abeyance, and it was possible to revisit the issue of names in a more tranquil and measured state of mind. I expressed the view that the meaning of names was essentially a matter of convention, a form of conditioning, and what sounded right in one time and place might differ in another context. An effort had been made to introduce a transition to the use of last names, but it felt awkward to everyone and had never really taken hold.

It was interesting to observe Krishnamurti's response. Gone was any sense of autocratic imperative, as had emanated from the school board. Gone, too, was any proposed solution. Rather, he simply brought into focus the essence of the issue as a factual matter. He asked if the students called me "David." He said it in such a way that we could all simply listen to how it sounded. He himself never addressed me in that manner—he called me "Moody" or "Mr. Moody," depending on the setting—and the way he employed my first name somehow sounded almost indecent.

In case there was any remaining doubt, before the conversation concluded he made his preferences clear. "Don't let them call you 'David,'" he said. It was not an order, but a word of advice. I was free to accept his counsel or not. In this way, his recommendation had far greater impact than if he had issued an ultimatum. Now, I had to take his advice into account and think the matter through for myself. I have no doubt that is exactly the result he intended.

Krishnamurti speaking in Ojai, 1979.

MELTDOWN

By observing him closely over the course of several years, one could discern that Krishnamurti formed strong impressions, both positive and negative, of the various individuals who came within his orbit. Anyone who imagines him as some ethereal mystic who bestowed a beatific affection equally upon all whom he met would be far from the mark. On the contrary, his perceptions of people were sharp and somewhat uncompromising and revealed a distinctive set of values and preferences.

One day, after a dialogue with teachers and others was breaking up, Krishnamurti took me aside and spoke in guarded tones. Without looking directly at a certain individual on the other side of the room, he said, "Do you see that man over there?" I nodded in the affirmative. "He is a *materialist*," he continued, almost as if he were diagnosing a psychological disease.

On another occasion, we were seated together at the lunch table, on a day when fifteen or twenty others were also present. There was a woman seated four or five positions to Krishnaji's left who was only just barely within his field of vision. He asked me quietly to observe how she was eating. I had never noticed it before, but her movements at the table were rather graceless, as she bent over her plate and shoveled large forkfuls of food into her mouth.

On yet another occasion, in the presence of a small group, I heard him recommend for dismissal a certain teacher with whom he had interacted numerous times. "She is *so* neurotic!" was his assessment.

As critical as he could be in certain respects, Krishnamurti's basic disposition was warm and affectionate, and there were some individuals on whom he looked with great favor. His chef and my good friend Michael Krohnen clearly fell within this camp, as did Erna and Theo Lilliefelt and, of course, Mary Zimbalist. He had a preference for people who were balanced, friendly, sensitive, well mannered, capable, serious, and with a sense of humor.

Another individual who fell firmly within the parameters of Krishnamurti's sense of approval was Mark Lee. He seemed to regard Mark as a kind of favorite son, one whose good deeds and qualities of character far outweighed any errors of judgment he might make.

The only indication I observed of a shift in this evaluation occurred one day at the lunch table, before the issues that arose in connection with names had come to any resolution. Mark used the word "dangerous" to describe the spirit of discontent that had seized the school community. He said it in passing, but Krishnaji focused on this word, challenged it, and forced Mark to consider its implications. The wave of protest might be considered unfortunate or even misguided, but he seemed to feel it was a legitimate expression of discontent. And to call it dangerous was to polarize the situation in a way that only added to the conflict.

Krishnaji could be somewhat demanding as a teacher, and he often corrected statements I made, sometimes rather sharply. But this was the only occasion in all my years at the school when I observed him do something similar with Mark Lee.

I was not privy to whatever conversations were conducted to determine Mark's fate; I certainly was not called in to consult with Krishnamurti about it, as I had been with Krause and Hidley. Instead, I learned from Mark himself that the tidal wave of rebellion had claimed him as its final victim.

I can only imagine the deep reluctance with which Krishnamurti and the trustees must have come to this decision. Mark was the primary pillar on which the school had rested from its inception. No other individual was so instrumental in every phase of the school's development, from the selection of students and staff to the fine details of landscape and architecture. Mark Lee was the very face of the school, its primary spokesman for daily affairs, and the glue whose attention held together all of its parts. His removal would leave a void of aching proportions in the very core of the enterprise.

Although he would remain in his post until a replacement could be found, as the days went by, the awful prospect of losing Mark's services began to sink in. It did not sit well in some quarters of the parent group, nor among several of the trustees. As a result, a new position in the foundation was carved out specifically for him. He was to become director of development, with fundraising and other responsibilities, but no lines of authority tying him to the school. All things considered, it seemed a fair and fitting outcome for a man who had devoted himself so fully to Krishnamurti's work.

Despite the turmoil that prevailed in the spring of 1984, the life of the school itself remained relatively unaffected. We continued to receive visitors for various lengths of time, including candidates for teaching and other positions. Among the applicants that spring was Terry Doyle, a bear of a man, tall, bearded, and physically fit. He had been involved in education for many years and had helped create a private secondary school in northern California. He had an easy, outgoing manner and was well versed in Krishnamurti's work.

Terry stayed at Arya Vihara for several days, and I spent a few evenings with two or three teachers, conversing with him. He had a friendly presence and just the right mixture of warmth and seriousness. I considered him a definite candidate for a teaching position or possibly a role as houseparent for our handful of boarding students. At the same time, however, I sensed in him a concealed current of high-strung unpredictability. I was prepared to hire him but would have been careful about giving him too much authority.

But Terry had caught the attention of the trustees as well. Theo Lilliefelt found a file of letters he had written to Krishnamurti in the early years of the school. In these letters, Terry expressed a comprehensive sensitivity to educational issues, and the trustees were rather impressed by the combination of the man and his written word. He was invited to the luncheon table with Krishnamurti and probably to the Lilliefelts' home as well.

In the aftermath of the decision to remove Mark Lee, Krishnaji asked me rather casually one day at lunch whether I could foresee any role for Terry at the school. I answered in the affirmative, but it was difficult to pursue the conversation further in that setting. After lunch, I followed Krishnaji out the back patio and asked him what function he envisioned for Terry.

He answered with a vaguely expansive gesture of the hand and a single word: "Everything." With that, he turned and headed across the lawn and into the orange groves toward his cottage.

And so, it came to pass that Terry Doyle was selected to serve as director of Oak Grove. A meeting with staff and trustees was called to announce the appointment, and one of the teachers, Richard Kortum, asked Krishnamurti whether this decision was not somewhat hasty. By that point, however, the die had been effectively cast, and only time could tell whether this particular soufflé would stand up after it had been removed from the oven.

In the meantime, a variety of loose ends remained to be wrapped up before Krishnaji departed for distant shores. The parameters of Terry's role had to be clarified, and my function needed to be realigned with his. Terry was to be director of the school as a whole, with special responsibility for the secondary section. I was to be director of the elementary school. The fact that the elementary section had eighty percent of the students was not considered an implicit contradiction in this arrangement.

Terry moved into his new role with energy and confidence. In a meeting of trustees and directors, he brought along a copy of Krishnamurti's formal statement of the *Intent of the School*, composed a few months before the school had opened. This document was a standard part of the school literature but did not function in any active way, and Terry's first initiative was to make it come alive. He said he wanted to post a copy of it on the front door of the school. In addition, he had the audacity to propose to Krishnamurti that the first sentence of the document—which to me was holy writ, immutable—be amended.

Even more remarkable, Krishnaji welcomed Terry's amendment and accepted it. In fact, this initiative precipitated a wholesale revisitation of the wording of the document. In the end, after meticulous attention to every detail, what emerged was a revised *Intent* with fresh energy. It was a most auspicious beginning to Terry's tenure.

—⁓—

In all the events that transpired during the course of that spring, Erna's voice and presence had seemed muted, if not absent altogether. The decisions that had been taken could hardly be interpreted as anything other than a repudiation of her influence. After all she had contributed to the work of the Foundation, she must have been smarting inwardly. In any case, that is how I viewed the events that followed, in which I felt she found a way to balance the books.

I had heard that Mark Lee was preparing a salary request for his new position, and I asked Erna if she would like me to propose terms for my revised role as well. She agreed that would be helpful. I jotted down some figures and had them with me during the meeting in which Terry suggested changes in the wording of the *Intent*. I passed my slip of paper on to Erna as the meeting broke up. By coincidence, Mark Lee did something similar at almost the same moment.

First thing next morning, I was called to meet again with the trustees in Mary Zimbalist's living room, where we had gathered the previous afternoon. I had a sense of foreboding that was amplified as I walked past Krishnaji's cottage. I heard him through his open window singing an ancient Indian chant as he went about his morning business. It was a sound I had never heard before, one with a haunting, melancholy undertone, reminiscent of a warrior girding himself for battle.

A somber atmosphere prevailed as everyone took their places. All the participants from the previous day were present. No one spoke until Krishnaji came in, seated himself, and began.

His comments were addressed to Mark and to me. He described the feeling of good will generated by the meeting the previous day, especially with all the attention to the foundational purposes of the school. In that context, he went on to say, the trustees had been rather shocked to receive, immediately after the meeting, salary requests from the two of us. Without using the word hypocritical, he strongly implied that our real concerns were evidently rather narrow and self-centered.

These remarks were delivered with a slow and deliberate solemnity. Each word fell upon the structure of my psyche like a hammer. No one in the room dared move or make a sound. As I sat leaning forward with my elbows on my knees, the cumulative comments caused my head to bow, and a tear or two fell upon the fabric of my pants.

I felt certain that Erna was the source of this condemnation but how she could have generated it from something so ordinary and matter-of-fact was beyond anything I could imagine. Perhaps there were some who felt I had escaped the events of that spring unscathed and deserved to be chastened as well. In truth, however, the entire sequence of events had enveloped me in stress that could no longer be contained. This dressing-down by Krishnamurti served to crystallize years of resentment at indignities endured, and I surrendered to a sea of self-pity.

The meeting broke up, and I bolted from the room. I made my way off the regular path through the orange groves to the back stairs of my apartment and crept inside through the back door. I went into the bathroom, closed and locked the door, and, as quietly as possible, allowed the emotional floodgates to let go.

After a few minutes, there was a knock at the bathroom door. I had hoped Vivienne hadn't been able to hear me come in the apartment, but she said Mary Zimbalist was on the phone, and Krishnaji had asked me to come back up to see him in his cottage. I managed to say that I would be there directly.

As I made my way up to the cottage, I passed Mark Lee and Terry Doyle sitting on the low stone wall surrounding the old pepper tree, chatting amiably. I didn't pause to acknowledge them, and they looked at me as if I were some kind of apparition. Perhaps Mark had not been too much affected by what had occurred—maybe it seemed to him less significant, after all that had already transpired.

I stumbled up to Krishnaji's cottage and knocked on the door. He opened it up right away, took one look at my face, and did something I found rather strange. He grasped my right hand in both of his and simultaneously turned his back on me. We stood like this in silence for several seconds. It seemed like an odd gesture, but it had the desired effect. I calmed down somewhat and recollected myself.

We sat together on the couch, and I began to find my voice. I tried to explain that Erna had *asked* for the figures I had given her. I must have still been fighting back tears because Krishnaji urged me two or three times, "Don't cry!" And at one point he added, "Do you follow? *I* want to cry!"

I had no idea what he meant by that or why he would want to cry; however, I took his advice and pulled myself together. I kept trying to explain that I felt Erna had pulled a nasty trick, but he did not want to hear about any of it. "Drop it!" he said. "Forget about it. It's over!"

Of course, it wasn't over for me, but the emotional meltdown had subsided, and I was able to lick my remaining wounds in private. I had long been of the opinion that Erna was rigid and negative in her thinking, but now I had reason to believe she was vindictive as well. There seemed to be a side of her that Krishnamurti was not aware of, and I began to weigh whether it was my responsibility to bring it to his attention.

———

A few days after the close of the school year, Terry met with Mark Lee and Erna in her office to discuss the budget for the following year. I was also expected to attend but did not have the stomach for it. I stayed in my apartment and hoped no one would care I wasn't present.

My phone rang half a dozen times that morning, but these were the days before answering machines, and I did my best to ignore it. I did not dare answer, for fear it might be a call to get up to Erna's office. She and Mark would probably have been fine without me there, but it was Terry calling, trying over and over to enlist my presence and support.

As he explained it to me later, Terry absorbed an eye-opening shock during the course of that meeting. They were reviewing teachers' salaries and benefits, and in that context Erna evidently discussed the teachers with an attitude of disdain. According to Terry, she continued in this vein at some length, in a manner that he could not comprehend, much less accept. Apparently, this meeting altered his perspective on the entire course of events at the school. He referred to it subsequently on several occasions.

Terry opened up the tenth year of the school with a meeting to which everyone was invited—parents, teaching and non-teaching staff, and students, young and old. It was held in the Pavilion late one afternoon toward the end of August, and the place was packed. The meeting had a grand, festive feeling. Terry, dressed in shorts and a t-shirt, held forth from one corner of the low stage, the tattoos on his forearms in full display, mementos from his days as a marine. His spirit was warm and expansive, and for that one moment, everyone felt like part of a big family.

I was impressed. It was just the kind of antidote to the more conservative style of Mark Lee and me that the school seemed to need. Terry was perfectly at ease and handled the meeting effortlessly, guiding it and allowing it to unfold. Best of all, from my perspective, he had no need to turn the spotlight toward me, and I was able to observe unobtrusively from my own corner of the room.

What remained to be seen was whether Terry's skill and judgment as an administrator would prove equally admirable. His expansive, all-inclusive instincts might be a liability in some contexts if not tempered by reflection and consideration of consequences. As it happened, he made two personnel moves that illustrated this point.

One of our best new teachers was Rupert Oysler, who had moved to Oak Grove from Tennessee. Rupert was a gifted graduate of Brown University, the elite Ivy League school. Among his other talents, he played the harmonica with exceptional flair and mastery. Rupert was married to Lynn, a woman some years his senior, and they had left behind in Tennessee her four children from a previous marriage, ranging in age from fifteen to twenty-three. Now that Rupert had a successful year at the school under his belt, they wanted to move the children out to Ojai, but they couldn't afford to accommodate them off school grounds.

Lynn asked Terry if he would let her children come stay at the school. It was the kind of request that Mark and I would have taken under consideration and probably decided against, on economic as well as other grounds. But Terry answered immediately in the affirmative. He didn't have to think about it. He found it unimaginable that the school would not extend itself in this way. Never mind that Lynn's kids were young adults, or that we hadn't met them or might not have room for them all.

Somewhat similarly, Terry wanted to hire as a history teacher a woman whose lifestyle was rather unorthodox. She was openly living with a married man who was still with his wife. The teacher and the man had had a child together who was being raised by all three adults. Terry not only hired the teacher but created a position for the man as school librarian, and he invited the whole family to live on school grounds.

I did not think such a living arrangement was an appropriate model at the school. If nothing else, it had to raise awkward questions in the minds of the students, and it seemed to me an open invitation to unforeseen trouble. But in these early days of Terry's tenure, I kept my apprehensions to myself and hoped that my reservations would prove to be misplaced.

Events came to a head unexpectedly, however, just a few weeks into the school term. Terry liked the idea of a school committee, provided it was composed of people at the school, rather than parents or trustees. He felt it was an effective compromise between autocratic decision-making, on one hand, and complete consensus on the other. The exact composition of the group had yet to be determined, but the probable lineup appeared to consist of Terry and me, the school business manager, and two rotating slots for teachers.

I returned to Oak Grove late one afternoon after a trip to Los Angeles and found Terry huddled in his office with two of the boys enrolled in the boarding section of the school. These boys were tenth graders, somewhat precocious intellectually but not given to good judgment in their behavior. Terry believed they could be cured by bringing them into the fold, and he was discussing with them whether they would like to serve on the school committee.

It did not matter to me what was Terry's rationale. I didn't care whether one or both boys would serve at the same time or whether they would be added to or replace one of the teacher positions—the whole idea was a complete non-starter. I objected categorically, and we agreed that he would take up the idea with the teaching staff at a meeting scheduled for the following day.

The teachers gave his proposal a decidedly chilly reception. No one spoke in favor of it. If Terry was really wedded to the idea, it soon became clear he was going to face an uphill battle. No one was openly hostile or confrontational, but Terry must have felt isolated at best, and perhaps somewhat humiliated. In any event, once the prevailing winds were apparent, he got up in the middle of the meeting and left the room.

Up to that point, it seemed that Terry was relishing his role in the school and navigating its various currents with skill and aplomb. Perhaps it is grasping at straws to suggest that the meeting with Erna during the summer colored his entire perception of the school. Nevertheless, it requires some stretch of the imagination to understand what motivated his action following his abrupt departure from the teachers' meeting. The next morning, he met with me in his office and announced that he had decided to leave the school. His reasons were not expressed with any clarity, but he could foresee that his marriage to the school was not a good match.

All that remained was for him to inform the trustees of his decision, but that would not be so easy. Erna and Theo were in England, attending an international conference of the trustees of the three Krishnamurti foundations. In order to implement his decision, Terry had to place a call to Brockwood Park. But he was not daunted even by that. He informed Erna by phone that he had decided to end his relationship with the school, effective more or less immediately.

Erna and Theo must have been not only shocked but mortified. They had probably spent some time informing their fellow trustees of events at the school and extolling the virtues of their new man on the job. For him to abandon his post less than a month into the school year represented a blow to their reputation for good judgment and left a messy situation that required their immediate attention. They had to make a spectacle of themselves, cut short their attendance at the conference, and hurry home.

Surely, Erna and Theo knew what they were going to do before they left England. There, they could consult with Krishnamurti and Mary Zimbalist and make whatever decisions were necessary. In any event, as soon as they arrived in Ojai, they asked me to assume Terry Doyle's position in addition to my own.

I weighed my decision for half a day, consulted with my wife and my conscience, and yielded to the flow of the river of events. Not without misgivings, but with no further negotiation or conditions, I accepted the mantle of sole director of the school.

Mary Zimbalist in her living room.

MORTALITY

Krishnamurti is regarded by many as a religious figure, but his actual stated philosophy is secular and psychological in nature. His aim is to elucidate the nature and dynamic structure of ordinary consciousness. His perspective is holistic and encompasses dimensions that philosophers call moral, ontological, and epistemological.

Epistemology is the study of knowledge. Because the transmission of knowledge is a primary function of education, assumptions about its nature must shape the quality of instruction. Krishnamurti's philosophy had a great deal to say about knowledge, and so it became the responsibility of a teacher in his school to consider how his observations should be reflected in the curriculum.

This, in any case, was my outlook at Oak Grove. In the earlier years of the school, problems associated with discipline and administration demanded attention and so distracted from the more interesting issues of curriculum and instruction. The principal advantage of my appointment as director was the luxury it allowed of focusing my attention as I saw fit, and that meant reflecting on the structure of the curriculum from the ground up.

According to Krishnamurti, knowledge is always limited in nature and in scope. However vast it may seem to us, knowledge is limited because it is the accumulation of the past. Psychological conditioning can be understood in terms of the received weight of individual and collective memory of the past.

Obviously, it is essential to employ knowledge effectively to function in daily life. Nevertheless, to see something new, we must put aside our accumulated knowledge and look with fresh eyes. This is especially important in human relationship, where memories of the other person tend to color and shape our perceptions, which leads to conflict.

Krishnamurti's perspective on knowledge is fundamentally revolutionary. While others may have put forth one point or another, he is unique in bringing these observations together in a coherent fashion and showing how important they are in the conduct of daily life.

Because his philosophy emphasized the limitations of knowledge, sometimes parents and others wondered whether his schools would effectively educate in the conventional sense. In our concern with ending conditioning, would we neglect to provide a standard course in academic instruction? Krishnamurti took pains to counter this view by emphasizing in the *Intent of the School* that academic excellence is "absolutely necessary." And yet, the concern persisted in many quarters.

As director of the school, I wanted to end that concern completely. My view was this: The insights provided by Krishnamurti's educational philosophy could be harnessed to achieve far *greater* academic gains than are possible through instruction by conventional means. The school should become known not in spite of its academic performance but because of it. Our students' achievement should be exceptional precisely because of our uniquely enlightened approach to classroom instruction. I made it my primary objective to implement this perspective and to build on that foundation to achieve our larger goals.

My first order of business, however, was to restore order to the difficult personnel situation that Terry had left behind. The man with two wives, one legal and one de facto, and their young child were due to move into quarters on the school property in the near future. The man had a long mane of yellow hair and drove a yellow Mercedes. It was bad enough that Terry had installed him as librarian in the jewel of the school buildings, but to have his unorthodox lifestyle on display twenty-four hours a day would have been intolerable.

There was a brief honeymoon period after I was appointed director, when Erna seemed for once grateful that I was available to help the trustees out of a difficult situation. She even made a little speech to the teachers and staff, urging them to give me their full support. I inwardly marveled at this, since I already had the teachers' support and knew it was hers that I would be needing sooner or later.

That time came even earlier than anticipated when I acted to annul the appointments of the librarian and the history teacher. Erna was dismayed that she would have to pay their salaries for a few months without receiving their services. Her husband, Theo, moreover, conservative in all his tastes, had taken an unaccountable liking to the librarian and bitterly resented my action. Even so, I never regretted it to any degree. I sensed that the man and his family would become the virtual image of the school, and to me he represented a caricature of the meaning of unconditioning, not the real thing.

—∿∿—

Krishnamurti's time in Ojai that year (1985) was cut short because of two trips he was scheduled to take to other parts of the country. The first trip was to Washington, D.C., where he gave a pair of public talks, and to New York, where he received an award from a committee of the United Nations. For a few days after he returned, I noticed him holding his hand to his side as he stood quietly at the end of the lunch line. It turned out his stomach had been uneasy while he was in Washington, and the aftereffects were still with him.

The sight of him in this condition, at age eighty-nine, precipitated thoughts of his mortality. For years, Krishnaji had reminded everyone that his days were numbered. "I am gone!" he admonished on many occasions. Perhaps the element of hyperbole in such expressions allowed us to take the idea with a grain of salt. But the sight of him holding his side in the lunch line gave it all a little greater sense of reality.

The second trip was to New Mexico, where he had been invited to speak to scientists at the Los Alamos National Laboratory. Several days before he left, he asked me over lunch what he ought to say to them. I don't think he really expected me to answer; rather, he was sharing what was on his mind and suggesting it was an interesting question to consider. It surprised me to see him in that state of uncertainty; on the other hand, his question indicated that he was weighing his remarks for days in advance.

—∿∿—

As the end of his annual visit came into view, I had to consider what life at Oak Grove would be like without Krishnamurti's participation. If he were gone, Erna's voice would prevail whenever she chose. I finally felt I had no alternative but to convey to him the depth of my misgivings about this prospect.

I met with Krishnaji in his cottage to spell out my concerns. I said that if he were not around, Erna was unlikely to keep me at the school for very long. She did not hold me in high regard and had no confidence in my abilities, I said, and in his absence, she would find a way to dispense with my services. In addition, she was not really serving his interests in her work for the foundation.

Krishnaji listened to all this rather calmly. He replied by describing in some detail how Erna had almost singlehandedly rescued his work from the machinations of Rajagopal. I said I did not question her dedication or her honesty, but all she really cared about were the financial condition of the foundation and its public image. In my view, she had little or no actual interest in the teachings.

Krishnamurti gathered himself and made a kind of pronouncement. "So you are informing me, in your official capacity, that Mrs. Lilliefelt is not supporting you in your work. Is that correct?"

I said that it was. I inferred from the way he phrased it that he would probably tell Erna some or all of what I had said, and he was giving me fair warning in case I wished to ask for confidentiality. But I did not take that path. I wanted him to do with my judgment whatever he felt was right.

A few days later, I was called to meet with Erna and Krishnamurti in Mary Zimbalist's capacious living room. Krishnaji repeated in her presence my apprehensions about her attitude toward me.

Erna refused to acknowledge in the slightest degree any doubt, reservation, misgiving, or animus whatsoever. Her stated position was that she totally supported me in my role.

I was unable to challenge her or to argue that she was being anything less than forthright. I found the confrontation rather intimidating, and Krishnaji went so far as to describe me as "inarticulate, for some reason."

The conversation drifted away from the matter at hand and began to revolve around the future prospects for the school. Krishnamurti admitted to doubts about whether the school would ultimately succeed. All his other schools were well established, with deep roots and secure prospects for the long term. If Oak Grove came to an unhappy end, he suggested, it would reflect adversely on his work. Erna said she had entertained reflections along a similar line.

I had to admit that I, too, had considered the possibility that the school would not succeed. Krishnaji and Erna, however, were quick to insist that I had no business thinking in that manner. Whatever double standard was implicit in their position was of no consequence to them. Their attitude was that, as the person in charge, I should never countenance such an idea—for me, failure must not be an option. It was their role, not mine, to entertain such doubts.

And so the meeting ended. There was a bond between Krishnamurti and Erna that was indissoluble, and I had no wish to persevere in that direction. I felt I had done my duty by offering my views. After that, events would have to unfold of their own accord.

———

Krishnamurti's apprehensions about the school were not based only on its uneven administrative history. Despite the demands on his schedule, he found time for a few meetings that spring with the teachers, and, evidently, he was not pleased with what he observed. A few of our most articulate teachers had left the school for various reasons, and of those who remained, many were content to sit back in the meetings with him and participate very little or not at all.

At one of the meetings, there was a young teacher sitting on the floor near Krishnamurti. She was wearing a dress with a long sash or belt, a narrow strip of cloth with an extra length of a foot or two. All through the meeting, she rather mindlessly rolled this cloth up and then unrolled it, perhaps as some kind of nervous habit or something to do with her hands.

Krishnaji mentioned this to me later in disparaging terms. He evidently regarded it as an action devoid of any self-awareness. In any case, he used it to illustrate a larger theme. "Cut out the dead wood," he admonished me.

I protested that it was difficult and painful to remove any member of the staff without very good cause. I suggested it might be possible, over the course of time, to confront some individuals with the fact that they were not well suited for the school, and encourage them to leave of their own accord.

"You mean, make it hot for them?" Krishnaji asked. "We tried that," he said. "It doesn't work." Evidently, he was referring to the early years of the schools in India, when he was more fully engaged in daily events. "You have to act," he concluded. "Cut out the dead wood."

—⁓—

An international conference of all the Krishnamurti schools was scheduled to take place the following December, at the Rishi Valley School in India. As the representative of Oak Grove, my participation was required. The foundation agreed to underwrite the expense of sending me and my wife. The plan was for us to go first to Brockwood Park, which I had never visited, and then to travel with the representatives from Brockwood on to India.

I confided to Theo Lilliefelt over lunch one afternoon that I was a little uneasy about travelling to India because everyone I knew who had gone there had contracted some kind of illness. A day or two later, Krishnamurti asked me rather solemnly if it was true that I did not wish to attend the conference in India. Evidently, Theo had twisted my words and conveyed them to him with the worst possible connotation.

I assured Krishnaji that I wanted to attend the conference. Any other course of action was unthinkable.

Brockwood Park.

CHAPTER TWELVE

INDIA

In the summer of 1985, I composed an essay outlining a blueprint for an entirely new approach to the school curriculum. I wanted to throw out the old categories and take a fresh look at the field of knowledge as a whole. English and mathematics are process skills that had to remain intact, in my view, but science and social studies represent categories of content for which the labels are shop-worn and vague, and the subject matter ill defined. The conventional disciplines, moreover, present to the student a fragmentary approach, as if they are separate islands in a sea of uncertainty. My aim was to present a new approach that would, in effect, uncondition the curriculum itself.

I took as my point of departure the nature of reality. The world we live in consists of three separate but interrelated realms or fields of activity, each with its own set of facts and operating principles. These are the physical, the biological, and the psychological. The physical consists of matter and energy, and the way these combine on earth to give us the oceans, the continents, and so on. The biological realm consists of life as a whole and the evolutionary principles that govern its development. The biological field is a by-product of the physical, but represents a unique set of phenomena governed by principles not present in the purely physical world.

Somewhat similarly, the psychological realm is a by-product of the biological world and is governed by a new set of principles not fully realized in biology. Psychology is primarily the province of man and is ruled by the activity of thought, although the borderline separating man from animal is not distinct, just as biological processes are not entirely distinct from their physical and chemical foundations.

The categories of knowledge, I maintained, should be organized in a corresponding fashion. In this way, the misleading labels of science and social studies are discarded, and the student is brought into contact with the substance underlying the categories of the curriculum. Science is a process, not an area of content, and to suggest that it applies only to physics and chemistry is misleading in the extreme. Social studies is a vague and dreary label and overlooks the fact that it is the individual who is the primary unit of psychological study. Moreover, science and social studies are conventionally treated in isolation. In the framework I proposed, the three realms would be seen in their mutual context and relationship with one another.

I developed these themes in an essay entitled "Toward a Comprehensive, Coherent Curriculum" and submitted it for publication in the *Journal of the Krishnamurti Schools*. The *Journal* was a newly created vehicle designed to share perspectives among the schools and to promote a greater degree of cohesion among them. The issue would be released in time to coincide with the forthcoming educational conference in India.

—⁓—

Vivienne and I arrived in London on our way to the conference late in November of 1985. A representative of Brockwood Park School met us at the airport and drove us eighty miles southwest to Bramdean. Our host there would be Scott Forbes, director of the school, a young man whose capabilities were as felicitous as the sound of his name.

Scott had come to Brockwood early in its formation and survived some turbulent years to become a personal favorite of both Krishnamurti and Mary Zimbalist. He was built like a boxer, medium height and broad shoulders, with rough, clean-cut good looks. He was warm and outgoing, engaging and well mannered. His tone of voice and style of interaction suggested a light, delicate touch, but underneath the surface, one could sense some of the qualities of a bulldozer: unwavering sense of direction coupled with iron determination.

Scott put us up for the first few nights in a room designed for a single student, into which a second bed had been inserted, leaving virtually no floor space for us or our suitcases. I was so annoyed I wanted to go stay in a hotel, but Vivienne calmed me down, and when we met Scott that evening he took pains to apologize. He assured us that the situation was only a temporary expedient necessary to make room for his father, who happened to be visiting from the States.

Our proper accommodations occupied the other end of the spectrum of hospitality. It was a beautifully appointed upstairs room, with a luxurious bed and comforter, situated next to Mary Zimbalist's quarters in another wing of the building. By the time we moved there, however, I had contracted a bad head cold with intense bouts of sneezing, now inextricably mixed into my memory of the place.

Brockwood Park could hardly have been more different from Oak Grove. Our students were mainly of elementary age; theirs were secondary. We were mostly a day school; they were entirely boarding. Our campus consisted largely of undeveloped land on which a few new buildings had sprung up; Brockwood was several acres of manicured lawns, stately trees, and lovely gardens surrounding an old English mansion, with a massive dining hall and kitchen, east and west wings, and endless nooks and crannies. The atmosphere there was one of good taste and old values, where intelligence could flower and beauty blossom in every corner or turn of the path.

Despite all this, I was eager to move on. The attractions of Brockwood Park, however fine, were no match for Krishnamurti himself. Vivienne and I were supposed to wait until the Brockwood contingent was ready and travel with them, but I had already arranged our tickets to leave for India a few days ahead of the others.

We flew to Bombay and then on to Bangalore, in the southern part of the subcontinent, where we were met by a wealthy industrialist who was a prominent member of the Krishnamurti Foundation India. He kindly welcomed us into his gated home, where we were fed and stayed overnight. The next morning, we were up early and set out on the two-hour drive to Rishi Valley, where Krishnamurti's oldest and most prestigious school was located. Our host's vehicle suffered radiator trouble on the drive, and we had to stop twice for improvised repairs. Nevertheless, we made it to the school just a few minutes into a meeting Krishnamurti was conducting with the teaching staff.

We were ushered into the back of a large room, crowded with a hundred or more teachers and staff, most of whom were sitting cross legged on the floor. They were all facing Krishnaji, who was also seated on the floor, leaning against a wall with his legs stretched out before him.

As soon as I laid eyes on him, I could sense something was gravely, indefinably wrong. His posture somehow lacked its usual grace and upright energy. I found myself fighting back tears.

The meeting proceeded as if all were normal. Krishnamurti's faculties were in no way impaired, and his voice was reasonably strong. After the meeting was over, he invited Vivienne and me to share some tea with him and two or three others. He showed us where his quarters were located in an adjoining room and asked us to come see him for breakfast the next morning. I had heard that Krishnaji was somewhat more relaxed and informal in India than in America, but discounted these reports as improbable or exaggerated. But to be invited to breakfast in Ojai would have been difficult to imagine.

When we arrived the next morning, Krishnaji was still in bed but sitting upright and alert. He asked us to sit near him and we were served a light meal. After we had eaten and the dishes were cleared, there was a moment of silence before he began to speak again.

"I may be going," he announced almost casually. It took several seconds for me to absorb the meaning of his words.

He explained that he was suffering from an ailment that his physician, Dr. Parchure, had not been able to diagnose. Further tests were going to be performed at a medical center in Madras when he arrived there in two or three weeks. In the meantime, his appetite was diminished, he was suffering persistent slight fevers, and his overall strength was declining, especially in his legs. In case there were any doubt as to the meaning he drew from this, he pointed to a wall on which were several shelves of his Indian clothes and suggested we select for ourselves any garments that might appeal to us.

Since he had left Ojai, he continued, he had visited Brockwood Park; the school at Rajghat, in the north of India; and now Rishi Valley in the south. And at each place, he had taken pains to ensure that the administration was on solid ground. Brockwood was in the firm and capable hands of Scott Forbes. Krishnaji spoke favorably and at some length of the newly hired principal at Rajghat, Dr. Krishna, a professor of physics from the University of Benares. Here at Rishi Valley, changes were also afoot. And some very difficult work lay ahead in Madras, involving the structure and leadership of the entire Indian foundation.

All in all, it was the picture of a man wrapping up the loose ends of his life's work.

We had been with him for the better part of an hour and, despite his condition, Krishnaji had done most of the talking. I was unable to speak. He invited us to join him on his afternoon walk and suggested we could drop in and see him again.

The campus at Rishi Valley was a village unto itself, some two or three hundred acres with every kind of building and facility required for a self-sustaining community. It was situated in a valley not unlike Ojai, with rocky hills rising on two sides, said to contain some of the oldest boulders in the world. Vivienne and I had spacious if somewhat primitive accommodations; we bathed with a bucket of warm water that was carried to us each morning. We ate well and slept well, and we had nothing in particular to do except drink in the surroundings and prepare for the educational conference scheduled to begin a week after we arrived.

After the significance of our breakfast with Krishnaji had sunk in, I went to see Dr. Parchure, whom I had met before in Ojai. He was a lively man, with excellent medical credentials and a keen interest in the teachings. I tried to pin him down regarding the status of Krishnamurti's condition. I asked why he was not being rushed straightaway to Madras or to the States for a complete evaluation. Dr. Parchure displayed no resistance to this idea but indicated that Krishnaji was committed to maintaining a certain schedule of activities for the next few weeks. He agreed that Krishnaji's health was declining and even suggested that he might no longer be able to walk in the foreseeable future.

I reported this conversation to Krishnamurti, who was somewhat taken aback at the prospect of not being able to walk. However, he did not seem to think that any medical intervention could cure whatever ailed him, and in any case, he would be in Madras fairly soon for further tests. The best I could do was point out that after he left India it would not be necessary to go back to Ojai by way of Brockwood Park, as was his custom, but that he could fly more directly via Singapore and the Pacific. He agreed this would be a good idea and gave me his passport and plane ticket so that I could make the necessary changes in his itinerary. His confidence in me at that moment seemed almost childlike, and I was flattered to be the custodian of his personal effects.

Before I had a chance to implement this plan, Scott Forbes and the Brockwood contingent arrived. Scott immediately got wind of what was afoot. He came to me without hesitation and asked me to turn over the passport and ticket to him. He certainly knew far better than I did the intricacies of travel in India, as he had been there many times before, and I somewhat reluctantly relinquished the documents.

In the days before the conference began, I had the opportunity to get acquainted with some of the individuals visiting from the various schools. Of particular interest was a young man who introduced himself one morning as I passed by the bench on which he was sitting outside one of the classrooms. His name was Sudanshu Palsule, and he was present because he volunteered for a few hours a week at a day school for under-privileged children in Bombay.

Sudanshu was tall and thin, with a full black beard and a liquid intelligence shining in his eyes. He had been reading my essay, "Toward a Comprehensive, Coherent Curriculum," and he wanted to tell me how much he enjoyed it. I could see at once that he was not fawning or seeking favors; his attitude was genuine and based on an intuitive appreciation for what I was trying to achieve. We struck up an immediate friendship.

It turned out that Sudanshu's regular job was as a professor of physics at the University of Bombay. He evidently had a brilliant academic future ahead of him, but his interest in Krishnamurti's work was strong. As I got to know him better, I asked if he might like to come to Oak Grove with his wife and young child to teach. To my delight, he answered in the affirmative. Sudanshu was just the kind of ally I would need to enact the radical premises of my proposed curriculum. I knew the immigration challenges would be formidable, but I resolved to do all in my power to bring him to Ojai.

Sudanshu was one of the few individuals in all the schools to comment upon my proposal. Another, somewhat curiously, was Krishnamurti himself. The morning that the conference was about to begin, I went up to his room to see how he was doing. To my surprise, he pointed to a copy of my essay sitting out on his dresser and said he had been reading it. He wasn't sure he understood it entirely, but from what he gathered he regarded it favorably. I was touched that he had read it at all, much less found grounds for approval.

Up to that moment, the conference had been planned to commence without his participation, perhaps in consideration of the uncertain state of his health. But when I saw him that morning, I could sense his energy and interest were still fully engaged in the work of the schools. I took that as an opportunity to invite him to join us that morning, even if only as an observer. He seemed pleased at the possibility and said he would consider my request.

This was the first educational conference of its kind, with representatives of all five of the Krishnamurti schools in India, as well as Oak Grove and Brockwood Park. As a result, it was natural for us to consider what we had in common. So the question with which the conference began was, "What is a Krishnamurti school?" This question was written prominently on a white board facing the audience.

The conference was held in a kind of outdoor pavilion. Eight or ten of us were seated on one side of a long table, facing an audience of two or three hundred teachers and other representatives of the various schools. Each of us at the table was supposed to speak in turn on the central theme and then take questions from the audience.

Just a few minutes into this process, Krishnamurti came down and took a seat in a chair a short distance away from the long table. He could see the question written on the white board and he listened respectfully for a few minutes. Then he politely asked if we would mind rephrasing the question to say, "What are these schools for?" He wanted the focus to be on their purpose rather than on his name.

However it was phrased, there was another issue underlying the conversation. Did it make sense for the several schools to differ significantly in their approach to education? Or should they, in essence, be one? And if they should be one, how could we bring about that result?

I suggested that we were, in fact, already one school, by virtue of our common intention—to transform consciousness, to uncondition the human mind. By recognizing our oneness as a point of departure rather than a destination, we could proceed to bring our respective approaches into harmony. If we started out as fragments, we would never find our way to becoming whole.

By the third and final day of the conference, Krishnamurti had still not participated to any significant degree, and I was afflicted with a growing sense of boredom and ennui. I went to see him in his room first thing in the morning and asked him to consider coming down and holding a dialogue with us. I had brought with me a question I had composed and left it with him. The question was this: Is a new mind the same as a good mind, a mind that is flowering in goodness? And what is the relationship of a new mind to an awareness of the wholeness of life?

A few minutes after I left his room, word came down that Krishnaji wished to speak with the conference participants. The seating was hastily rearranged, and loudspeaker and recording systems were rounded up and put into place. Krishnamurti brought with him the paper on which I had written the question, and he opened the meeting by asking me to read it aloud. The dialogue proceeded from there without much regard for the substance of my question, but it had already served its purpose.

That conversation on December 17, 1985, was the last dialogue that Krishnamurti conducted with teachers. It is included in the book *The Future Is Now*.

—m—

In keeping with Krishnaji's more relaxed and accessible ways in India, a sizable retinue accompanied him on his afternoon walks. At four or four-thirty, he would emerge from his quarters to find a small posse of us waiting to follow him around the spacious property. He had cultivated the school's development for half a century, and he couldn't help but admire its food and flower gardens, banyan trees, practical innovations, and rugged natural setting. But the day finally arrived when he walked the grounds of Rishi Valley for the last time.

If he experienced any degree of sorrow or regret, he gave no sign of it. He was certainly aware of the implications, and he allowed Scott Forbes to photograph him along the way. Nevertheless, he walked with a spring in his step and took everything in with evident appreciation, as was his custom. Certainly, there was a current of nostalgia in the air, but one could not be sure if it was a projection of some kind or an objective actuality.

Vivienne and I had been in Rishi Valley for three weeks. The conference was over, and we had no further business to conduct in India. Nevertheless, the KFA had decided that we should take in as much as possible, and so we were to follow Krishnamurti to Madras for another two weeks. We were housed in the compound known as Vasanta Vihar, a few gated acres on the edge of the city. The headquarters of the KFI were located there, and the spacious lawns and open courtyard were sufficiently large to accommodate an audience of several hundred for Krishnamurti's public talks.

Krishnaji's room was located in the building adjacent to ours, and it was a little easier than in Rishi Valley to keep an eye on who was coming and going and to find opportunities to drop in and see him. It was so different from Ojai, where everything was done by appointment. His manner was usually cheerful and welcoming, despite his illness and the demands on his time. His room was not especially large, but it was uncluttered, with open doors and plenty of natural light, and it had a warm, spacious feeling.

One morning, as we sat together on the rug on the floor of his room, Krishnaji asked me who would hold the schools and foundations together after he was gone. It did not dawn on me until later that he may have been inquiring obliquely whether I might take an interest in such a role. It would entail visiting each of the schools in India, England, and America, as he did, on a yearly basis, and making sure that each was proceeding in a manner consistent with his intent. I suggested the names of a couple of individuals I thought might be suited for this function, but it was hard to imagine anyone who could fill these shoes.

As we sat on the floor together on another occasion, he asked why none of the schools had really fulfilled its deep intention. The schools in England and America were comparatively young, but in India, two of his schools had been in operation for nearly half a century. As good as they were in many respects, there was no evidence yet, in either students or teachers, of any real transformation of consciousness.

He suggested a possible reason by quoting an old Indian saying: "Under the banyan tree, nothing grows." Where there is a man whose influence is as wide and deep as the shade of a banyan tree, it may be more difficult for those in close proximity to him to realize fully their own creative potential. Only after such a man dies might it be possible for them to flower in their own right.

—⁓—

Not far from the compound at Vasanta Vihar was the very beach at Adyar where the fourteen-year-old Krishnamurti had been "discovered" by Charles Leadbeater. There he went now for his afternoon walk along a two-mile promenade, accompanied by a dozen or more of his friends and associates. The pace was rather brisk for a man of ninety, never mind one suffering from a serious illness. Scott Forbes usually walked with him shoulder to shoulder, the two of them like the head of a comet, with the rest of us fanned out for twenty or thirty yards behind. Krishnaji was quite a sight, with the wind whipping his white hair behind his head and the beach and big waves crashing on one side, while the glorious sun set on the other.

How poignant it was to observe a man at the end of his long life striding along the very beach where he had played in his youth.

—◦—

One morning, toward the end of our stay in Madras, I crept up the stairs to Krishnaji's room and found the door open, as I had hoped. He invited me in, and we sat together one more time on the rug. In that relaxed and contemplative moment, he unexpectedly asked me if it would facilitate my work at the school if I were to be put "completely in charge." I had not heard him use that phrase before, but he said he had been discussing it with Scott Forbes, and he asked me to consider its implications.

Then he turned and gestured toward a small dresser at the side of the room. On its surface was a letter he had received recently from Terry Doyle. Something about the letter and the way he referred to it made it seem radioactive. He said he could not divulge its contents, but he asked me if I thought that Terry was an objective, reliable witness of events. I later learned that in this letter, Terry had laid out his assessment of what ailed the Oak Grove School. He said that the root of the problem lay in the attitudes and personality of Erna Lilliefelt.

With the benefit of hindsight, it seems apparent that the coupling of "completely in charge" in the same conversation with the letter about Erna was no coincidence.

———

In addition to the visitors he received and the business he was conducting with the members of the KFI, Krishnamurti was scheduled to give three public talks on the grounds of Vasanta Vihar. One morning, a few days before the talks began, I saw him and noticed a discoloration high on his forehead, evidently a bruise of some kind. He explained that in the night he had gotten out of bed and lost his balance, scraping his head against the wall. It was evidently another symptom of the advancing nature of whatever ailed him.

I came to see him again the day before the talks and found him resting in his bed in the middle of the afternoon. I urged him again to cancel his talks and go directly back to the States. He considered it for a moment but then said that was impossible. He had already cancelled talks scheduled for later in Bombay, and too many people had travelled too far to Madras to cancel on such short notice. He seemed to be at peace with this prospect, but he closed his eyes and lay back on his pillow to let me know it was time for me to leave his room.

Vivienne and I both became rather ill toward the end of our stay in Madras. We were advised that the rash on Vivienne's chest might be chicken pox, and if it were so diagnosed, she might have to stay there in quarantine for eight weeks. As a result, we cut our visit short by a few days and returned home a little earlier than originally planned.

We departed Vasanta Vihar one evening immediately after Krishnamurti's last public talk. The place was not large enough for the audience of more than a thousand that crowded together and spilled into the street to hear him deliver the final talks of his long life. In one of the talks, he reflected on the meaning of death; he said that death cuts us off from all our attachments with "a very, very, very sharp razor." He asked if it were possible to bring that razor into every day of our lives and live without attachment to anything whatsoever.

Vivienne and I arrived at LAX late in the evening after the interminable flight from Madras via Frankfurt. I had a bad flu and fever and no idea how we were going to find our way back to Ojai. By an act of great mercy, Mark Lee and his wife were waiting at the airport to ferry us home. The States never looked so good to me—the broad, orderly freeways, the cleanliness, the sense of predictability—and the minute we got home we collapsed into bed for a long sleep.

Last public talks in Madras (1985).

CHAPTER THIRTEEN

WINTER, 1986

K rishnamurti returned to Ojai by way of Singapore with Scott Forbes, Dr. Parchure, and Adelle Chabelski, a friend from California. When he arrived, he was still able to walk, and we had a few days in which to hope that he might yet make a recovery. However, Dr. Deutsch, his American physician, soon established a diagnosis of pancreatic cancer. From that day forward, it was apparent that the future course of events was ineluctable.

The sense of inevitability was amplified when Krishnaji lost the ability to walk. The strength in his legs simply ceased to be sufficient to support his diminishing weight. Mary Zimbalist made arrangements to keep him as comfortable as possible in a hospital bed in his room in Pine Cottage. By the third week in January, it was apparent he would not be getting up again.

I was ill with a spiking fever and a purple rash from head to toe for nearly two weeks after we returned from India. In this interval, Krishnaji deputized Scott Forbes to investigate the state of affairs at Oak Grove and report to him what remedies, if any, were required. Scott met with the teachers collectively and struck up a rapport with them. They were supportive of my role, and their voice formed the basis of Scott's recommendation.

Over the course of the next thirty days, I was able to visit with Krishnamurti for short periods of time on half a dozen occasions. In order to do so, it was necessary to penetrate the various filters imposed by the nearly round-the-clock presence of Mary, Scott, and Dr. Parchure, not to mention nurses and others who were present intermittently. When I succeeded, I generally found Krishnaji awake, in good spirits, and lucid. He was usually lying on his back in his bed, but he would open his eyes to see who had come in and offer some word or gesture of welcome.

As soon as I was well enough to visit him in his room, Krishnaji took the occasion to inform me of certain developments. He said he had been talking with Scott and Mary Zimbalist, and they had agreed that I should be put "completely in charge" of the school. It was the same phrase that he had used in my last conversation with him in Rishi Valley.

They had discussed the matter with Erna, he said, and she had accepted their recommendation. All that remained was for me to confirm this result with her. He evidently wanted me to initiate a conversation with Erna in which she would acknowledge that she had agreed to this formulation of my role.

During that period, I was accompanying Erna once or twice a week on her early morning walks, and she had ample opportunity to discuss with me any changes in my position or status at the school. When she took no initiative in this direction, I broached the matter delicately and asked her what she understood of what Krishnaji had proposed.

Erna kept her gaze fixed on the ground. She expressed a perfunctory acknowledgment of what had transpired but without any enthusiasm or elaboration of what it might mean. Rather than press the issue, I allowed the matter to rest.

The next time I saw Krishnaji, the first thing he said was, "Have you spoken with Mrs. Lilliefelt?" I told him I had, and that we had agreed that I was to be completely in charge of the school. He seemed to breathe a sigh of relief. But after a moment of silence, he asked, "Have you told the school?" I said I had not told anyone.

"No, sir, you must," he replied. He seemed to be of the opinion that it was up to me to make the matter public. I assured him I would do so.

Erna probably felt railroaded by circumstances into agreeing to something whether she liked it or not. I can well understand any reluctance to challenge or contradict Krishnamurti on any matter of substance at that time. When he asked me if I had discussed the matter with her, I was able to say that I had, although I refrained from divulging any of the reservations I felt. But when he urged me to announce the result to the school, I lacked a sufficient sense of conviction to act upon his request. And when he later inquired if I had made that announcement, I took the course of least resistance and told him I had, when I had not.

I would have ample opportunity in the future to reflect on the consequences of my lack of action. In truth, none of this ever held much sense of reality for me. It was all too little, too late. Among other things, it did not seem like a matter for me to raise with Erna, but for her to raise with me. In any case, I felt she was capable of expressing outwardly whatever the situation required, and if she harbored inner reservations, time was on her side. Whatever leverage I could bring to bear would be child's play compared with the resources she could marshal after Krishnamurti was gone.

—⁓—

In view of Krishnamurti's condition, most of the prominent members of the English and Indian foundations had gathered in Ojai. These included Mary Cadogan, the author and secretary of the English foundation; Mary Lutyens, his lifelong friend and biographer; Pupul Jayakar, the intellectual powerhouse and confidante of Prime Minister Indira Gandhi; Pupul's nephew, Asit Chandmal; Dr. Krishna, the newly appointed head of the school in Benares; and perhaps a dozen others. Even as he lay in his bed, unable to walk, Krishnaji held two or three meetings with many of these individuals in order to iron out final arrangements for the copyright for his life's work.

I knew these meetings were taking place but was not informed at the time about their substance. I could not help but wonder if I should have been included. My concerns were laid to rest the next time I found my way into Krishnaji's room. As soon as he saw me, without any preamble, he remarked, "Sir, don't feel excluded!" Although I knew exactly what he meant, I was baffled how he knew how I felt, for I had not said anything to anyone. "Oh," he explained, "I can feel it."

If Krishnaji, even in his illness, was sensitive to my emotional vibrations, he was even more aware of the collective energy of all those who had come from afar to be present in his final days. Evidently, that energy did not sit well with him. One morning, as I wandered up towards his cottage, I encountered Dr. Krishna striding along the path with a sense of purpose. He told me that my presence was required in a meeting that would be held in Krishnaji's room within the hour.

Gathered there together were all the dignitaries who had come from distant continents to say farewell to Krishnamurti. He was sitting up in his bed and he spoke for several minutes. The pitch of his voice occupied a higher register than usual, but his speech was clear and his mind was lucid.

He began by describing the current state of his medical condition. There was no doubt that his end was near, but its timing could not be determined with any accuracy. In the meantime, he was confined to his bed, unable to walk or look after his own basic needs. When he contemplated this prospect, his voice broke, and he nearly succumbed to tears. But he told us to disregard that reaction, as it was merely the response of the physical body to the prospect of indefinite confinement.

Then he moved on to the main business at hand. As dear as all those present were to him, he could feel them waiting for his departure, and it was interfering with his ability to rest. There was nothing further to be accomplished by their staying in Ojai. The copyright issues had been settled. It would be best if all those present who did not actually live in Ojai would say good-bye now and make their way back to their homes.

Evidently, the copyright issue was rather sensitive, for Krishnamurti took this occasion to implement one final action before he brought the meeting to a close. He told Scott Forbes to get a hand-held tape recorder that was kept nearby. He asked Scott to speak into it and to vow that he would preserve the recordings that had been made and ensure that the decisions taken would be implemented. Scott did so, but Krishnaji was not satisfied.

"You must *swear* it," he said. The scene had an uncanny resemblance to the ghost of Hamlet's father swearing his son to action. Scott repeated his vow, this time with more conviction, and the meeting came to a close.

The following day, I drove Mary Cadogan to the airport in Los Angeles. She said she had left Krishnaji with a written question, and she wondered if he would find the energy to address it. She had asked what becomes of the energy that is Krishnamurti after the body ceases to function. Does it continue in some fashion, whether through reincarnation or in any other form?

Krishnamurti's answer was delivered a day or two later into the hand-held recorder. He was unequivocal: nothing whatsoever would continue after the body was gone. He added, for good measure, that anyone who said it was possible for a wise man to will his own death and leave the body at a time of his choosing did not know what he was talking about.

Krishnamurti used the occasion to make a number of other provocative comments. No one in his lifetime had ever understood the sheer physical magnitude of what had transpired within him— "like a twelve-cylinder engine." And no one alive had fully lived or understood the teachings.

———

One morning, after all the guests had left town, I cautiously opened Mary Zimbalist's front door, found that the coast was clear, and crept into Krishnaji's room. I pulled up a chair to the side of his bed and asked how he was feeling. He spoke in a voice barely more than a whisper and said he had very little energy but otherwise was feeling all right.

I asked him if his illness were not some kind of mistake. He looked at me and asked what I meant. He had been so physically fit all his life, I explained, and his work was not yet finished. Although I did not say so, I was inquiring whether there were forces in the universe charged with protecting him, and if so, had they failed in their function.

"No, sir," he replied. "There is no mistake." He explained that his body had been cared for like a thoroughbred horse for a long time; nevertheless, it was inevitable that sooner or later one part or another would wear out.

He seemed to suggest that he was now just waiting to depart, and I asked if Dr. Deutsch could not simply amplify the morphine drip into the intravenous solution that kept him fed and hydrated. He shook his head slightly and said that would look like suicide, and he did not want that associated with his death.

I asked if he was still learning. I used the word deliberately, as I knew it held special meaning for him. "Oh, yes," he said, "that is the problem." He said his mind was learning day and night, even in his dreams. He did not say why that was a problem, but I gathered he meant he wanted to express what he was seeing but no longer had the energy to do so.

It would be several days before I had an opportunity to see Krishnamurti again. By then, each day might be his last, and the situation was so tenuous that I did not dare risk intruding at some inopportune moment. I expressed my reservations to Scott, who said he would let me know if a good moment arose. When his call came a day or two later, I made my way up to Pine Cottage with the feeling it might be for the last time.

The house was entirely quiet when I let myself in, and no one was in sight. Krishnaji lay motionless on his back in his bed when I entered his room. His slight, diminutive figure seemed to be melting away. He hardly had the energy to acknowledge my presence, but he gestured slightly toward a chair next to his bed and I sat down. He seemed to be too weak to speak, but he held out his hand as if for me to take it, and I did. He held my hand in his on his chest, and then he lay still, eyes closed, once again.

After a moment, I gathered the courage to speak. "I'm sorry I haven't been able to come see you," I said. I was leaning slightly over his bedside and watching his face intently, but he remained completely still.

I paused every few words to keep my voice from breaking. "But I want you to know… that I think about you… all the time… and I remember… everything you have told me."

Krishnaji still did not speak or register any facial expression, but he responded by increasing the force of his grip on my hand with surprising strength. It was a gesture more meaningful, perhaps, than anything he could have said. In that grip, I felt the vital pulse of his energy still flowing, still communicating his passion to uncondition the mind of mankind.

He held my hand in this manner for several seconds. Then we sat together in silence for a long moment. Then I quietly said good-bye and took my leave.

———

The intensity of Krishnamurti's grip on my hand stayed with me throughout the remainder of that day and all through the next. The following morning, I went out early to meet Erna on her walk but found her in her car instead of on foot, headed toward Pine Cottage. She was dressed in her most severe business suit, and her face was pale. She pulled over and motioned for me to get in the car.

She told me that Krishnamurti's breathing had gradually slowed throughout the previous evening, and that he had passed away ten minutes after midnight. She had just gotten off the phone with a reporter from the *New York Times* and was headed up to Pine Cottage to help look after final arrangements for the body.

Krishnamurti had left instructions that he did not want his body to be put on display after his death. For this reason, I was hesitant to follow Erna into Pine Cottage, and she did not invite me to go in with her. I watched her walk alone up the stone pathway and go inside. Then I turned and made my way through the orange groves back to my apartment.

At the end of that long day, Mark Lee kindly came to see me and told me what had transpired. The body had been washed and laid out in fresh sheets on the bed. Several people were on hand to witness the expression on Krishnamurti's face.

Shortly after 8:00 a.m., the body was transported to a crematorium, accompanied by Mark, Mary Zimbalist, Scott Forbes, Asit Chandmal, and Dr. Parchure. The process of cremation entails a heat sufficient to burn bone, but evidently, it is not an exact science. At some point, the oven was opened up to ascertain whether the process had been completed, and Mark got a glimpse inside. There he saw the searing image of Krishnamurti's skull consumed with fire.

Krishnamurti, White House Hotel, London, September, 1968.

ENDGAME

Krishnamurti held that teaching is the highest profession. What exactly he meant by "highest" was not entirely clear, but he contrasted it with the profession of soldier, which represented the other end of the spectrum.

One day at the lunch table, the conversation turned to the various professions and the effect they have on the individuals who enter them. Krishnaji maintained that there exists a "stream" associated with each profession, representing the collective thought and activity of all the people participating in that line of work. To enter into any given profession was to enter into that stream, and so to be shaped by its values and customs.

In his schools, the role of the teacher went far beyond that associated with education in the conventional sense. The teacher was charged with the radical responsibility of unconditioning himself, as well as the student, and by this means transforming the consciousness of humanity. By any standard, this could only be an audacious proposition. On the other hand, it was the natural and inevitable outcome of his overall philosophy.

Krishnamurti himself was a teacher of the highest order. Annie Besant had trained him from an early age specifically for the role of World Teacher, and although he disbanded the organization she created for him, he never disavowed that role. His talks from the public platform and his published writings were collectively referred to, with his consent, as "the teachings," although he preferred to call them not the teachings of Krishnamurti, but rather the teachings of life.

If there was a single, central fault line that separated my overall outlook on the school from that of Erna Lilliefelt, it revolved around the relative roles of teachers and parents at Oak Grove. In my view, the teachers had the greatest possible responsibility, and they required a commensurate degree of authority in order to carry out their work. Within the overall framework of the intent of the school, I felt the teachers should play a central role in all major decisions, including hiring and firing of teachers and staff, determining educational policies, and so forth.

The parents, by contrast, were clients of the school, and it was a privilege for their children to be enrolled there. Families whose values and behavior were not consonant with the intent of the school might not be invited to remain. The teachers were ultimately responsible to make assessments of this kind.

Erna's view was diametrically opposite my own. As far as I could ascertain, her outlook was shaped by financial considerations, although other factors probably entered in as well. On the accounting balance sheet, the parents were sources of income, and the teachers represented the largest category of expenditure. All other issues seemed to be viewed through the prism of those calculations.

Whatever the basis for her judgments, she consistently elevated parents to a role of supervisory oversight in the school, a policy with which I was fundamentally at odds. This only began with Drs. Krause and Hidley; after they made their exit, she introduced others in similar roles. The successors to the two doctors were more circumspect in their actions, but over time, I found them almost equally onerous.

———

In the weeks after Krishnamurti's death, Erna appeared to make an effort to work with me in the manner he had requested. She had heard reports from India that I had made a good contribution to the educational conference, and when she conveyed that to me, she seemed both pleased and surprised in equal measure. She wrote in a memo to the bookkeeper at the school that I was now "in complete charge" of the school, although she buried that phrase in the third of several paragraphs and offered no explanation of what those words might mean.

She even invited me to attend a meeting of the trustees at which foundation business unrelated to the school was discussed. This was unprecedented in my experience. The directors of the schools in England and India were automatically members of their respective foundations, but Erna held that the legal structure of the KFA made that impossible here.

In the meeting I attended, Erna raised the question whether the final recorded pronouncements of Krishnamurti on his deathbed could be considered an authentic part of his teachings. She asked whether those recordings should be kept under permanent lock and seal or even destroyed. Since Krishnamurti had insisted in everyone's presence that Scott Forbes vow to preserve these recordings, her proposal struck me as impractical as well as irresponsible. I said that if the KFA destroyed those tapes, it would become the primary act for which they would be remembered forever.

I was not invited to attend any further meetings of the KFA.

By the summer after the 1985–86 school year, Erna's attitude toward me had reverted to its normal condition. She nominated to the board of the KFA two individuals who were parents of students currently enrolled in the school. My relationship was neutral or favorable with the majority of parents, but the two whom Erna selected for membership on the KFA held specific grievances against me, and I interpreted their appointment as laying the groundwork for my dismissal.

In October of 1986, as the new school year was getting under way, I decided to bring matters to a head. One morning, while I accompanied Erna on her walk, I told her that her overall relationship with the school was "destructive." I said her attitude was overbearing, judgmental, and very negative and was having unfavorable consequences for the school's development.

From that day forward, it was probably only a matter of time until Erna could marshal the resources to terminate my services, and I gave her no shortage of ammunition with which to work. There were eight trustees, and she would need a majority to fire me. Three of these were parents of students in the school, and I had conflicts with each one over issues related to their children. One even threatened me with a lawsuit over a memo I wrote defending my actions related to her daughter's transfer to another school. In a meeting with the trustees called to discuss this issue, I told Erna, "Maybe I had better get a lawyer," and she replied, "Maybe you had." She later claimed she was joking, but at the time she said it, there was not an ounce of mirth in the room.

In mid-February, the trustees debated whether to fire me. The three who were parents were fully prepared to let me go, and Erna and Theo were as well. That left three who might have been more neutral. One of these sided with the majority, while the remaining two argued in my favor. Of these two, one was Mary Zimbalist, whose approval meant more to me than the disapproval of all the others combined.

Largely because of her influence, the trustees restrained themselves and ended my responsibility for the secondary school only. Mary Lou Sorem was appointed to take my place there, and I remained in charge of the elementary section. Mary Lou had been with the school for several years and was attractive, personable, and detail-oriented. Her most outstanding characteristic, in my mind, was that she never contributed a single question or comment in any of the teachers' meetings she attended with Krishnamurti. In this, as in some other respects, she was the antithesis of me.

It had been less than a year since the death of Krishnamurti. In the weeks and months that followed, I tried to convince myself that peace and order had been restored to the situation. As time went by, however, this fiction became increasingly impossible to maintain. Erna had moved her office out of the KFA facilities into the administrative building of the school, and her presence there on a daily basis was unnerving in itself. In addition, she began to attend all of the weekly meetings of teachers and staff. In one of these, she made the declaration that, "David Moody is not a director." The overt meaning of this statement was rather obscure, since it was manifestly contrary to fact, but its larger implication was unmistakable.

Even so, I continued to believe it might be possible to remain in my post. Then the trustees mailed out a questionnaire to the various families that had left the school, for whatever reason, within the last several years. I was not consulted on the reason for or the wisdom of this idea, much less on the nature or wording of the questions asked. Three of the ten questions invited comment on the quality of the school administration. Erna kept the results in a file in her office and shared them with me only selectively.

After this occurred, I concluded that discretion was the better part of valor, and I approached Erna with a proposal. I offered to resign my position in exchange for a one-year paid sabbatical to finish my Ph.D. I added that I would like the opportunity to return as a teacher of mathematics after that year was finished. I did not want to sever my connection with the school entirely and hoped this proposal might salvage some kind of continuing relationship. Erna said she would present my idea to the trustees.

The teachers met to discuss whether they could intervene to reconcile the situation. Some even contemplated resignation. I pleaded with them to do everything in their power to create a stable situation and minimize the effects of my inevitable departure.

I later learned that Theo Lilliefelt said the teachers' continued support for me indicated I had "brainwashed" them and that he had called me "a Svengali."

A few days later, the trustees presented me with a document outlining the terms of my departure, and I was asked to sign it on the spot. The document was in the form of a letter accepting my resignation and granting my sabbatical year, but it specifically added that I would not return to the school in any capacity. I protested this element and said it was not at all what I had proposed. Erna told me it was necessary to insert that clause "for legal purposes," but assured me that the directors in the future would be free to hire me if they saw fit.

I asked the other trustees if they would confirm what Erna had just said. Two or three of them nodded in the affirmative, and I proceeded to sign the document.

For the whole of the next school year, I continued to teach one math class at the middle school level. I did so as a way of earning part of my continuing salary, as well as to assure the trustees that I could function as a teacher without being involved in the administration of the school in any degree. At the end of the year, the directors proposed re-hiring me as a math teacher, but the trustees replied in writing that such an action was forbidden by the terms of my departure. Erna's verbal assurance to the contrary was nowhere to be seen.

And so, my association with the Oak Grove School came to an end.

The question remains whether events might have turned out differently had I fulfilled my promise to Krishnamurti to inform the school, while he was still alive, that I was now "completely in charge." It is impossible to know how this would have affected the ultimate outcome. In view of what did occur, however, I am satisfied that no such pronouncement could have changed the course of events. The forces aligned against me were too deep and too strong, and had been waiting for too long to have their day.

Nevertheless, I found it remarkable that Krishnamurti was able to propose such a change at the very end of his life. I had tested those waters just the previous year and found him firmly in Erna's corner. To reverse course in the final days of his life represented an exceptional degree of flexibility and demonstrated anew the meaning of the unconditioned mind.

Krishnamurti with David Bohm, 1983.

CHAPTER FIFTEEN

DAVID BOHM

K rishnamurti did not consider himself to be an intellectual, but throughout his lifetime he formed close relationships with individuals whose intellects were of the highest order. These people were thoroughly exposed to his philosophy and personality, and each came away with the greatest regard for his capacity and his contribution.

First among these was Annie Besant, who raised Krishnamurti from the age of fourteen and looked after his education. Annie's career was extraordinary for the courage she displayed from an early age, as well as for the range of her accomplishments and the power of her voice, both in writing and from a public platform. Krishnamurti jeopardized her confidence in him when he disbanded the international organization she had created specifically to advance his work. In spite of this, to the end of her life, she looked upon him with the highest degree of admiration and respect.

Next in this line was Aldous Huxley, with whom Krishnamurti became close friends during the nineteen forties. Huxley's mind was encyclopedic; and, as demonstrated in *Brave New World* and his many other books, the power of his intellectual vision was world class. During the war years, when Krishnamurti was confined to Ojai, the two men visited one another regularly and shared long walks and a deep rapport. Huxley contributed the foreword to one of Krishnamurti's early books, *The First and Last Freedom*, in which he presents a rather detailed analysis of Krishnamurti's work. He says that Krishnamurti offers the reader "not ritual, not a church, not a code, nor uplift or any form of inspirational twaddle," but rather "a clear contemporary statement of the fundamental human problem, together with an invitation to solve it in the only way in which it can be solved—by and for himself."

Pupul Jayakar also deserves to be mentioned in this context. She was an author and recognized authority in fine Indian art, as well as a high governmental official and close confidante of Prime Minister Indira Gandhi. She was instrumental in the development and operation of the Krishnamurti Foundation India, and after his death, she composed a biography that examines his life and work in all its dimensions.

Perhaps the brightest star in this particular pantheon, however, was theoretical physicist David Bohm. In the early nineteen fifties, Bohm made important contributions to the foundations of quantum theory. Among those who are interested in Krishnamurti's work, Bohm is understood as an important scientist, but there are few who fully appreciate the magnitude of his work. Bohm refined the meaning of the very equations that govern quantum theory, and in so doing, he altered the course of physics itself.

Quantum theory deals with the behavior of matter at the subatomic level, in the land of the electron. In that realm, many of the features associated with ordinary reality seem to be absent.

Among these is the simple principle of cause and effect; in the land of the electron, causation itself appears to be missing in action. Prior to Bohm, the prevailing interpretation of events at the quantum level—in a radical departure from all other fields of study—held that what happens there occurs strictly at random.

In a pair of seminal papers published by *Physical Review* in the early nineteen fifties, Bohm demonstrated that the mathematics that governs quantum theory could be interpreted in such a way as to preserve the principle of causation. This revolutionary contribution went right to the core of quantum theory and has not been refuted to this day. The standard model continues to interpret events at the quantum level in random terms, but Bohm's alternative stands as an enduring testament to the fact that all is not yet settled at that level. The cover story of the February 1993 issue of *Scientific American* is devoted to alternative interpretations of quantum theory, and Bohm's view is spotlighted as preeminent among them.

Bohm was a native-born American and protégé of theoretical physicist J. Robert Oppenheimer, an association that landed him in trouble with the House Committee on Un-American Activities. He appeared before the committee twice in 1951, where he courageously refused to answer several questions on grounds of principle as well as the Constitution. As a direct result, he lost his professorship at Princeton University, although his refusal to answer was later upheld in federal court. He discussed the matter with Albert Einstein, his close friend, and the two agreed the political climate was so poisoned that Bohm should take a position outside the country. He accepted a professorship at the University of São Paulo in Brazil, whereupon the State Department revoked his passport, restricting his travel and effectively terminating his

American citizenship. In this manner, Bohm became another casualty of the McCarthy era.

In 1955, Bohm took a position at the Technion, Israel Institute of Technology in Haifa, where he met his wife, the artist Sarah (known to friends as Saral) Wolfson. Two years later, he accepted a position as research fellow at the University of Bristol, and in 1961 became professor of theoretical physics at Birkbeck College in London, where he remained for the rest of his life.

The textbooks Bohm authored on quantum theory and the special theory of relativity are considered models of clarity and classics in their field. Over the course of his career, however, the theoretical position he had established early on acquired larger and deeper dimensions. His original analysis of quantum theory developed into a more fundamental notion about the very fabric of physical reality, as well as its relationship with consciousness. He elaborated the notion of an "implicate order" that underlies all phenomena and imparts a quality of wholeness to the entire universe. A collection of his papers on this subject was published by Routledge in 1980 as *Wholeness and the Implicate Order*.

As a result of these investigations, Bohm was interested in the study of man as well as nature, and the relationship between the two. A fundamental principle of quantum reality involves an intrinsic connection between the experimental observer and the subatomic particles being studied—in the land of the electron, the very act of observation has an effect upon the objects observed. And so, when Bohm's wife, Saral, ran across a book whose author proclaimed "the observer is the observed," she brought it to her husband's attention. The book was *The First and Last Freedom* by J. Krishnamurti.

Bohm recognized the significance of Krishnamurti's work, which paralleled his own in certain respects. He sent a letter through Krishnamurti's publisher to see if it would be possible for the two men to meet. They did so in London in 1961 and began a dialogue that continued for two decades. Over the course of those years, Bohm became Krishnamurti's most important collaborator. The two men seemed to recognize in one another a mind of profound intelligence, originality, and dedication to truth. The record of their long dialogue is preserved in several volumes, encompassing all their mutual interests in consciousness and reality. Among these titles are *Truth and Actuality, The Ending of Time*, and *The Future of Humanity*. In the final years of Krishnamurti's life, their conversations diminished in frequency, but the two men maintained a deep, mutual respect to the very end.

Bohm was instrumental in the establishment and development of Brockwood Park, the boarding school for secondary students in England. For many years, he and his wife spent their weekends there, a steady resource of wisdom and guidance for students and staff alike.

In his conduct of group meetings, Bohm was the antithesis, in some respects, of Krishnamurti. The latter was quick to correct errors of language or logic, and he engendered an atmosphere that was austere. By contrast, Bohm was like a shy and friendly uncle, endlessly tolerant of all the imperfections in the family. It was said by some who knew them both that Krishnamurti began his answer to every question with "no," whereas Bohm answered every question with "yes."

After Oak Grove opened in 1975, David and Saral travelled to Ojai and visited for several weeks every year. They stayed in an apartment at Arya Vihara that came to be known as the Bohm flat, and opportunities to forge a friendship with the renowned scientist were plentiful. Bohm usually presented himself in a professorial coat and tie, but his manner was warm and accommodating. His conversational style was very precise but soft-spoken and unassuming, laced with humor and flashes of insight and originality.

In my last year as director, I arranged for Bohm to conduct a weekend seminar at the school, open to the public. With a little moving of furniture, one end of the spacious library could accommodate an audience of fifty or sixty. For eight or ten hours, spread out over several sessions, Bohm spoke and took questions from the audience. The topics and issues he covered overlapped with Krishnamurti's teachings, but represented Bohm's particular perspective, expressed with his own characteristic language and colorful, illuminating metaphors.

After I left the school, a few of Bohm's friends formed a committee to continue these seminars in Ojai for several years. The fees generated were sufficient to cover his and Saral's travel expenses, with a little left over. The seminars were recorded, transcribed, and edited for the printed page, and are available through the University of Michigan dissertation services. The 1990 seminar was published by Routledge under the title *Thought as a System*.

And so, I was able to enjoy Bohm's company for several weeks each year long after I left the school. When he was in Ojai, I made my way up to the Bohm flat around 4:00 on most afternoons, and Saral would serve tea and cookies while Dave and I chatted. Then he would be ready for his walk, and the serious conversation would begin. Our regular route took us up a road with a mild incline, half a mile to the Thacher School, a boarding school, where there were paths without cars, broad fields, and views of the valley below.

Our walk would usually take an hour or an hour and a half, and there was never a shortage of conversation. Bohm's appetite for philosophical discussion was inexhaustible. He liked to quote an aphorism that he attributed to Hegel: the owl of Minerva (Roman goddess of wisdom) flies at dusk. And so, we would walk and talk into the twilight, examining at our leisure every puzzle of consciousness.

I recorded a few of my conversations with Bohm and transcribed them for my own interest. One of these focused on his scientific work, as I tried to make his overall perspective on physics accessible to a general audience. This dialogue was published privately in pamphlet form under the title *Physics and the Laws of Nature.*

Many of our conversations revolved around the nature of Krishnamurti as a man and the significance of his work. Now that Krishnamurti was gone and his work could be assessed in its entirety, what was the overall value of his contribution? If no one had undergone the transformation he described, could his work be considered a success?

Bohm regarded Krishnamurti's teachings as fundamental and probably without parallel. At the same time, he felt that they were missing some essential element or not entirely properly expressed. He felt that Krishnamurti was given to excessive use of words such as "all," "never," "every," and "always"—terms that carry an absolute, unyielding quality. Bohm said that the overuse of such words was counterproductive to the clarity Krishnamurti wished to impart.

I asked if Krishnamurti's work was lacking a kind of "fine focus" that would depict the dynamics of consciousness with a greater degree of detail and nuance. Bohm accepted that manner of characterizing the situation. He clearly believed Krishnamurti had made an enormous contribution, but also that important work remained to be done.

Many have wondered whether Bohm himself represented an individual who had undergone the kind of psychological transformation described by Krishnamurti. His ability to express the meaning of many points in the teachings certainly suggested that possibility. The fact that he could converse with Krishnamurti on an equal footing, as displayed in their published dialogues, also supports such an interpretation.

Despite these indications, it was very clear to me that Bohm did not regard himself as having undergone the kind of change described by Krishnamurti. The fact that no one at all had done so was the implicit or stated premise of innumerable conversations between us. I often urged Bohm to compose a book expressing his views of the psychological field, but he insisted he was not able to do so because his own understanding remained incomplete. He regarded himself as remaining caught in a fundamentally conventional structure of thought and identity, notwithstanding his facility for describing that structure in the most creative and illuminating terms.

David Bohm died of heart failure in 1992 at the age of seventy-five. He was a man who combined great warmth and humility with an intellect whose dimensions can hardly be grasped. A few years before his death, a volume of essays in his honor was published under the title *Quantum Implications*, and the list of its contributors reflects the range and depth of his contribution: Richard Feynman, J. S. Bell, Eugene Gross, J. P. Vigier, and Karl Penrose, among the physicists; and Maurice Wilkins, Ilya Prigogine, and Karl Pribram, among those from other fields.

Before he died, Bohm completed a comprehensive textbook summarizing his overall perspective on theoretical physics: *The Undivided Universe: An Ontological Interpretation of Quantum Theory*. But in his hours away from the university, it was the work of Krishnamurti to which he returned right until the end. The night before he died, he and Saral watched a videotape of one of Krishnamurti's talks, and when it was over, he remarked, "We should have kept on talking." Saral took solace in the thought that now the two men could resume their conversation without end.

Krishnamurti with Oak Grove students, 1979.

THE INSIGHT
CURRICULUM

The tale is told of Archimedes, the most illustrious mathematician of antiquity, whose king presented him with an unusual challenge. The king had received as a gift from a neighboring monarch a crown, purportedly made entirely of gold. But the king was somewhat suspicious of the crown's provenance, and he wondered whether silver or some baser metal had been mixed in with the gold. Without actually melting it down to determine its composition, how could it be ascertained whether or not the crown was entirely gold? The king turned to his most brilliant subject, Archimedes, for a solution to this puzzle.

Archimedes examined the issue from every angle without success. Finally, in frustration, he decided to put it out of his mind temporarily and relax. That afternoon, he asked his servant to draw him water for a bath, and as he settled into his tub, he watched the water level rise and almost overflow. In that moment, he saw the solution to the problem of the composition of the crown: if it were submerged, the amount of water the crown displaced could serve to measure the density of the material it was made of, and therefore reveal whether or not it consisted entirely of gold.

Archimedes leaped from his tub and ran outside in naked exuberance. "Eureka," he cried—Greek for "I have found it!"

This story, although possibly apocryphal, has come to be considered paradigmatic of the process known as insight. It is a process recognized and studied within the discipline of psychology, although less so within the field of education. Insight, moreover, is a key component of Krishnamurti's approach to understanding consciousness, especially in the dialogues he conducted with David Bohm. As such, it provides a point of contact between his philosophy and the findings of academic research.

Bohm sometimes illustrated the nature of insight with a story about a rabbit and a fox. On several occasions, the fox had chased the rabbit through the field where it lived, but each time the rabbit escaped by diving into a hole in the ground at the last minute. As the rabbit had several holes, the fox was always a little too late. But one day, he saw the rabbit run into one hole, only to emerge a few minutes later from another. At that moment, the fox realized that all the holes were connected through tunnels underground. So he covered up the other holes with dirt and waited until the rabbit finally emerged from the one that remained.

The school of psychology known as Gestalt was the first to give systematic attention to the process of insight. One of the salient features of visual perception is the tendency to organize information into coherent patterns, in which each piece has its place in a larger framework. This tendency is so natural and deeply embedded in our visual apparatus that it often goes unnoticed, but it can be brought into focus by means of certain figures in which the visual pattern is subject to change.

Below are three figures that illustrate this process. In each case, what appears at first to be a simple and unambiguous representation is susceptible to a sudden and unexpected reorganization of the visual information. The transformation of perception that occurs in observing such figures is similar or analogous to what takes place in the process of insight.

Sometimes, insight involves putting together or creating a pattern of information where previously none had existed. A textbook case involves a chimpanzee who is kept in a large play area with a variety of objects and toys at his disposal. A psychologist comes in and suspends a bunch of ripe bananas from a cable several feet off the ground. The chimp tries to reach them by standing on a box, but the bananas are too high. He tries to knock them down with a stick but is still unable to reach them. He is about to give up when it suddenly occurs to him to stand on the box and reach for the bananas with the stick at the same time. In a moment of insight, he has organized the elements of his situation into a new pattern that enables him to achieve his goal.

Perhaps because the essential quality of insight is not verbal, it has been used as a means of studying intelligence in animals. A crucial feature of intelligence is the capacity for self-awareness. This ability can be ascertained in animals by means of a mirror. When presented with its own reflection, a gorilla or chimpanzee will soon realize that it is looking at itself. This awareness is sometimes tested by painting a red dot on the animal's forehead. Upon observing the dot in the mirror, the self-aware individual will generally touch its hand to its forehead to see what is there. Dolphins also have this capacity, although the dot has to be placed elsewhere on its body in order for the dolphin to twist to observe it directly. A dog or cat, by contrast, will not recognize itself in a mirror. A cat will shadow-box with its image in a mirror for minutes at a time or scrape with its paw at the glass in an effort to push away the intruder.

The relevance of insight to human intelligence has been less thoroughly explored. Psychologists have instead debated questions such as whether, or to what extent, intelligence is a matter of "nature or nurture," genetic inheritance or the product of social and cultural factors. The predominant assessment holds that intelligence is largely a matter of inheritance, with some supplementary influence from events following conception. But in Krishnamurti's view, intelligence is a far more malleable quality than is currently recognized. Moreover, it is to be distinguished from the intellect, rather than identified with it.

Krishnamurti regarded intellect as a matter of thought and analysis operating within the field of knowledge. Intelligence, in his view, is a far more potent, subtle, and fluid capacity, one associated with perception, with seeing what is. It is precisely the freeing of the mind from the limitations of knowledge that allows intelligence to flower. Insight, the sudden perception of something new, represents the purest form of the operation of intelligence.

After I left Oak Grove, I returned to the School of Education at UCLA to undertake the research for my doctoral dissertation. I explored a series of findings in the field of science education, including the cognitive obstacles students encounter in learning basic scientific principles. From topics as diverse as gravity, electricity, the laws of motion, the shape of the Earth, and the principles of evolution, studies indicate that some concepts are particularly difficult for students to grasp. Research reveals that students approach these concepts with preconceived notions that are at odds with the scientific outlook. Such preconceived notions evidently represent formidable obstacles to overcome by ordinary means of classroom instruction. The reasons why, however, have not been clearly established.

My research suggested that this issue could be understood with reference to the process of insight. Drawing in part upon Gestalt psychology, I defined insight as a rearrangement of the relationships among a set of facts and ideas held in the mind of the learner. In other words, certain concepts in the sciences are not possible to grasp merely by a process of accretion or incremental addition to the student's pool of knowledge. Rather, such concepts require that an existing set of relationships among facts and ideas be broken down and restructured to conform with a new pattern of understanding. I set forth these views in a chapter of the volume *Mapping Biology Knowledge*, published by Kluwer (now Springer) in 2000.

Illustrative of this field of research is the way young children come to terms with the received information that the Earth is round. Hills and valleys notwithstanding, children expect the Earth to be predominantly flat, as was widely believed in ancient times. And so, when they are told that the Earth is round, they typically attempt to reconcile that information with their preconceived notion of flatness by imagining the Earth as round like a pancake—that is, both round and flat at the same time. Numerous studies of young children across cultures have documented this finding.

To come to terms with the notion that the Earth is round like a ball, not a pancake, is challenging on more than one account. First, it is necessary to envision the sheer magnitude of a planet on which a curved surface can be perceived locally as essentially flat. Beyond that is the question of gravity and what happens to people on the other side of the planet. To a child, gravity is associated with the direction of down, which is understood to be an invariant feature of the universe. What is to prevent people on the other side of the planet from falling off?

To understand that the Earth is spherical, therefore, requires a rearrangement and correlation of several elements. The size and shape of the planet, the notion that up and down can be relative to location, and the nature of gravity must all be brought into focus as part of a single, coherent pattern. Such an understanding has the quality of insight. It goes beyond the mere addition of a piece of factual information ("the Earth is round") and entails the perception of a set of relationships among several diverse elements in a larger whole.

A somewhat more sophisticated case of a similar process involves the explanation for the origin of seasons. Most students, and many adults, subscribe to the notion that seasons are caused by the planet's changing distance from the sun. The Earth's orbit is somewhat elliptical, and summer and winter are believed to correspond to the variations along that curve. In a videotaped study of Harvard students, several graduating seniors articulate this view with characteristic Ivy League self-confidence.

It requires a complete transformation of perception to understand the true explanation for the origin of seasons. The slightly elliptical nature of the Earth's orbit around the sun has nothing to do with it. The seasons are, rather, a by-product of the fact that the Earth's axis of rotation is tilted relative to the plane of its orbit around the sun. As the planet travels around the star, the tilt in its axis of rotation causes the southern and northern hemispheres to be exposed for longer and shorter periods of sunlight. To perceive the relationships among the Earth, its axis of rotation, the plane of its orbit around the sun, and the seasons, entails a new perception of a pattern of conceptual elements. It requires an insight.

The research I conducted for my doctoral dissertation examined high school students' understanding of the process of natural selection as the basis for the theory of evolution. Most students subscribe to a pre-Darwinian view of the process by which evolution occurs. Several decades before *On the Origin of Species* was published, the eminent biologist Jean-Baptiste Lamarck had proposed that species evolve by virtue of the efforts and activities of individuals. Each individual transmits to its offspring the changes it has achieved during its lifetime. The giraffe stretches to reach the highest leaves and so passes on to its descendants its elongated neck. Although this view has been thoroughly discredited in scientific circles, it remains alive and well in the preconceived ideas that high school students bring to their biology class.

In order to understand the scientific view of this matter, students need to consider an entirely different constellation of elements. Natural selection has nothing to do with the inheritance of characteristics acquired by individuals during their lifetime. It is the result of mutations and other sources of genetic variation within a population of individuals and the differential effects of these variations upon reproductive success. To achieve this understanding, students need to adopt a new perspective on the relationships among a diverse set of elements. They need to have an insight.

The field of science education is replete with comparable instances in which student understanding is impaired by the active interference of preconceived ideas. Researchers and educators have struggled to find ways and means of overcoming such ideas, which are often rather robust or well entrenched in students' cognitive frameworks. Perhaps what needs to be understood, by students and educators alike, is the necessity for insight, for a complete transformation in perception of relationships, rather than the mere addition of a new fact or concept, in order to achieve the scientific view.

This understanding of what is required would be greatly facilitated by an entire strand of the curriculum devoted to the cultivation of moments of insight. Not only science education, but mathematics, history, language arts, and social studies are each fertile sources of this type of cognitive challenge. Rather than regarding such situations as obstacles, a progressive and enlightened school could treat them as unique opportunities for the kind of learning associated with insight. To do so would, as a byproduct, help restore to the educational process some of the joy of discovery too often missing from the modern classroom.

An insight curriculum would be uniquely suited to the kind of education proposed by Krishnamurti. Such a curriculum would entail not only an organized catalogue of concepts and principles associated with insight, but also include attention to the kind of state of mind most conducive to that result. Krishnamurti frequently pointed out that knowledge, which is the repository of the past, often functions as an impediment to the perception of something new. Psychological freedom, in his view, consists, in part, of freedom from the past, freedom from the known, which is the prerequisite to transformation. Insight, in short, is closely related to the process of unconditioning, and so an insight curriculum may serve to align and correlate the academic curriculum with the deeper purposes of a Krishnamurti school.

Until such a curriculum is fully developed and ready for use, interested readers may wish to explore the nature and quality of insight for themselves. One way to do so is to consider a puzzle whose answer is accessible to understanding but just out of reach. Such a puzzle might involve the nature of the moon's orbit around the Earth. We know that the apparent revolution of the sun around the Earth each day is just an illusion caused by the Earth's rotation on its axis. But the moon really does revolve around the Earth. Is that what we are observing when we see the moon move across the sky during the course of any given night?

And what accounts for the phases of the moon? When the moon is full over the skies of North America, is it also full in South America or in India? Why does the moon repeat its phases on a monthly basis?

To see the answers to these questions requires the perception of a set of relationships involving the Earth and its rotation, the moon and its orbit, and the position of both with respect to the sun. Such a perception has the quality of insight. It is of a piece with the kind of deep understanding that Krishnamurti invites us to bring to bear upon the contours of our consciousness.

Krishnamurti, Holland, 1926.

IMAGES AND
REFLECTIONS

Throughout his adult lifetime, Krishnamurti underwent a series of personal experiences that are very difficult to interpret or understand. These began with the sequence of events that occurred in 1922, shortly after he and his brother Nitya first came to Ojai. Among these were an intermittent but chronic pain in the back of the head and neck and episodes of an hour or more in which his normal personality seemed to leave his body, while a childish persona remained until he returned.

For most of his life, Krishnamurti went to some lengths to keep these experiences from becoming known publicly, evidently for fear that their disclosure might distort the understanding of his message. In 1975, however, he authorized the publication of a biography in which these events were described in some detail. Composed by Mary Lutyens, a well-regarded author and his friend for many years, the volume was entitled *Krishnamurti: The Years of Awakening*, and it covered the years from his birth until 1933. A subsequent volume, *The Years of Fulfillment*, described the continuation of such experiences and made their meaning one of the central issues of her work. In that context, Lutyens raised the question, "Who or what is Krishnamurti?" She evidently considered these episodes crucial for understanding his nature as a person.

Lutyens put her question to Krishnamurti himself and solicited whatever information or insights he could provide. The question was received without resistance, but the answers were not very illuminating. Krishnamurti said that he could not describe his own essential nature. "Water cannot know what water is," as he put it. He did not mind reviewing a variety of hypotheses and examining their respective merits. At the end of it all, however, the question itself remained unanswered.

Perhaps of greatest interest about his responses was the lack of reference to the personal experiences that precipitated the question for Mary Lutyens. Evidently, he did not regard these episodes as relevant, even though they were what triggered the interest of his biographer. This suggests that Lutyens's question may have been somewhat misconceived, notwithstanding Krishnamurti's willingness to entertain it.

I raised these issues with David Bohm, and we examined them at some length. In his view, the essential nature of Krishnamurti as a man can never be understood by anyone who has not undergone a somewhat similar transformation of consciousness. This would include, at the least, a deep and penetrating insight into the nature of thought and its implications for personal identity. In the absence of such an insight, any description of Krishnamurti's outlook and awareness would have little meaning.

Despite any misgivings we may have about the question Mary Lutyens posed, it does remain intriguing, as well as unanswered. As a result, we are led to ask what the observations contained in this volume may contribute to its resolution. One of the salient features of my relationship with Krishnamurti was the almost total absence of any evidence pertaining to any unusual psychological events or states of mind he may have experienced. In all our hours of interaction, he never of his own initiative alluded to any of it in the slightest degree.

I felt it would take unfair advantage of my proximity to him to inquire into his personal experiences and therefore restrained myself, with two exceptions. One of these has already been described. In a private conversation, I asked if it was true (as reported in *Tradition and Revolution*) that he had never experienced the ordinary sense of personal identity. He confirmed that this was the case, although he did not seem to attach any great significance to it.

On another occasion, in a quiet moment at the lunch table, with only a few people present, the conversation turned to some issues associated with Theosophy. The Theosophical Society had predicted the emergence of a new World Teacher, a role for which Krishnamurti was specifically selected and groomed. In addition, the Theosophists held that there exists a kind of pantheon of "ascended Masters," somewhat supernatural individuals, enlightened to various degrees, who inhabit an ethereal realm and look after events on Earth.

Although he had severed all relationship with Theosophy fifty years earlier, I asked Krishnamurti how he regarded this aspect of its philosophy—did the Masters really exist? The question was germane to the experiences Mary Lutyens described because some of the "out-of-body" episodes seemed to suggest the involvement of such individuals. When I put this question to him, he hesitated before offering a brief, quiet answer, without elaboration—"too concrete."

I found it remarkable that his answer was anything less than a total repudiation of the concept of the Masters. On the contrary, he left the door open for some form of energy or intelligence not known to our ordinary understanding of the world. Evidently, the Masters represented a kind of personification that Krishnamurti did not accept; but he seemed to acknowledge that there is something out there, nevertheless.

Beyond Krishnamurti's personal experiences, there remains a larger question about his identity that Mary Lutyens largely overlooked. Krishnamurti's stated philosophy is devoid of any reference to Theosophical principles or ideology. Nevertheless, his career represents an uncanny fulfillment of the Theosophical prophecies made for him at an early age. Anyone who regards Krishnamurti's teachings as profound and original must consider this question: how is it possible that this outcome was in principle predicted by Besant and Leadbeater many years before any discernible evidence of it existed?

From a logical standpoint, three possibilities suggest themselves for consideration. To anyone who accepts Theosophical doctrine, the answer to the riddle is rather self-evident: Krishnamurti's career is the perfect confirmation of the truth of Annie Besant's vision. This interpretation, however, entails accepting the whole structure of speculation associated with Theosophy and so is unacceptable to a scientific temperament.

A second explanation is that the prediction of Krishnamurti's future, proclaimed when he was fourteen years old, represented the model of a self-fulfilling prophecy. In this view, the act of selecting a boy for this role and grooming him assiduously, as Annie Besant did, provided in itself sufficient preparation for the outcome that occurred. While this explanation at least offers a rational model to account for events, it still must be regarded as implausible at best. This view rests on the assumption that any adolescent with appropriate qualities of intelligence, sensitivity, and receptivity could have achieved a similar result.

To anyone familiar with the scope, the depth, and the beauty of the teachings, such an explanation is not satisfying. Not one man in a million, or a hundred million, could produce this body of work, no matter what the nature or quality of his upbringing. It is like suggesting that a Mozart or an Einstein could be produced simply by predicting and training a fourteen-year-old for such a role. Although more appealing than the Theosophical account, this explanation still defies credibility.

A third possibility is that the success of the Besant-Leadbeater prophecy was merely a matter of luck or coincidence. On this account, they struck it rich, rather in the manner of someone buying a winning lottery ticket. If Krishnamurti's talent was one in a million, or one in a hundred million, the chances of selecting him for his role in advance would, in fact, approximate those of picking a lucky lottery number. It is improbable in the extreme but not impossible.

To the rational mind, this third explanation is no more appealing than the first two. Collectively, the three explanations fall short of any satisfying account for the sequence of events. Nothing in Mary Lutyens's biographies, nor in the teachings themselves, and certainly nothing in my observations, offers any real clue to this most improbable outcome. Even more than the riddle of Krishnamurti's personal experiences, the uncanny success of the predictions made for him at an early age simply defy any reasonable analysis.

Although it is interesting to speculate about Krishnamurti's personal identity and the sources of his psychological insight, these issues have no bearing on the validity of his teachings. The truth of his observations about the landscape of consciousness is wholly independent of the individual who articulated them. Krishnamurti took pains to point out this elementary fact. He refused to be accepted as an authority, and the teachings were not offered on that basis. On the contrary, as he constantly reiterated, his work had no meaning or significance apart from what the individual listener could see or understand for himself.

With this in mind, we might suggest an alternative to Mary Lutyens's question. Instead of asking, "Who or what was Krishnamurti?" we might consider asking, "What is the essential nature of the teachings?" Where in the overall spectrum of human endeavor do they lie? Is his work best understood as a species of spiritual philosophy? Was it a contribution to some existing world religion or even the beginning of a new one? Or is Krishnamurti better understood in a vein that encompasses Kant, Hegel, Freud, Jung, Wittgenstein, Maslow, and Piaget—that is, as a source of secular insights and observations regarding thought, identity, and consciousness?

Perhaps some perspective on this issue may be gleaned from another student of Krishnamurti's work. Radhika Herzberger, the daughter of Pupul Jayakar, was director of the Rishi Valley School at the time of the educational conference that I attended there. Radhika's impressions are apparent in an introduction she composed to *The Future Is Now*, a volume containing Krishnamurti's final talks and dialogues. She describes Krishnamurti's moods, activities, and interactions with nature during the last year of his life.

In the course of a dozen pages, Radhika makes mention of the Buddha no less than seven times, and on each occasion, she draws some parallel with Krishnamurti's life or activity. She does not come right out and say so, but the implication is apparent: Krishnamurti was the Buddha, or was like the Buddha, or is best understood in a context whose central element is the Buddha. Whichever alternative any given reader may infer, the universe of possible interpretations of his work remains implicitly circumscribed by this comparison.

And so we may ask, where in the broad spectrum of inquiry does the work of Krishnamurti actually lie? A content analysis of his stated teachings, performed at any stage of his career, would show without question that the scope and substance of his work falls within the parameters of secular psychology. His exposition from the public platform is devoid of any reference to supernatural goals or guidance, or otherworldly experiences. It is devoted almost exclusively to the step-by-step delineation of the contours of daily consciousness of the normal human mind. Since his published remarks on these issues are voluminous, there can be no question whether sufficient evidence exists to establish this conclusion.

This raises, in turn, the question of why Krishnamurti's work is not widely regarded in this light. Several factors contribute to that result. Krishnamurti never had any association with a university or organization recognizably part of the established community of intellectual discourse. Nor were his language and subjects of discussion chosen to conform to the interests of that community or to contribute to its dialogue. His perspective on psychological issues, moreover, was holistic, encompassing the entire range of human thought, emotion, motivation, desire, action, and responsibility. The absence of a fragmentary focus is probably sufficient in itself to exclude him from the mainstream of psychological discourse.

In addition, Krishnamurti's exposition of the nature of consciousness was not divorced from his overall attitude toward human conflict and suffering. His was not a dry, analytical description but rather one informed by a deep awareness of the moral dimensions involved in human behavior and relationship. In this respect, as well, he removed himself from consideration by the established guild of social scientists.

If Krishnamurti's work is not easy to categorize in terms of content or substance, it is even more so with respect to what the social scientists refer to as "methodology." By what method, mode, or procedure did Krishnamurti arrive at his conclusions? What is the analytical, or empirical, or other basis for his claims? Do his means or methods conform to the canons of scientific procedure? If not, how can his statements be taken seriously, even if they do fall within the parameters of secular psychology?

In this, as in many other respects, Krishnamurti's work is both original and transparent. Had he tried to sidestep this issue, it would indeed count as a weakness in his presentation. On the contrary, the question of method is at the forefront of his exposition. Like the social scientists, he considers it crucial, however different from theirs his approach may be.

Before describing his approach, it may be helpful to consider the context in which the field of psychology operates. Not only psychology, but all the social sciences are preoccupied with the endeavor to establish their scientific credentials. The successes of the physical sciences in the last few centuries have left the social scientists hungry for a methodology that can achieve comparable results. For this reason, the philosophy of behaviorism reigned supreme for half a century. Remarkably for a theory of psychology, behaviorism regarded the mind as off-limits to scientific procedure and held that only the observable stimulus and response of a living organism could or needed to be taken into account.

A revolution in the field of psychology occurred in the nineteen seventies, when the operations of thought, or "cognition," were readmitted into the domain of scientific inquiry. To be sure, the return of the mind into psychological studies was permitted only under certain circumstances. The statements of "subjects" were accepted as reliable evidence only in highly controlled experimental conditions. This innovation nevertheless represented an admission that the narrow procedures formerly considered inviolable were simply not adequate to explain the wealth and variety of subjective phenomena.

What is still anathema to the accepted conventions of social science is for the individual conducting the investigation to report upon his or her own state of mind. A strict separation between the observing investigator and the subject under study must be maintained at all times. This restriction is required in order to enable other investigators to replicate the obtained results.

Krishnamurti rejected this requirement absolutely. Although he was receptive to the necessity for logical rigor, his approach to psychological understanding remained a matter of the inspection of one's own state of mind. To be sure, he also rejected "introspection" on grounds that it was an analytical dissection of internal events. But if that term could be taken in a purer sense, to refer to the direct and immediate observation of one's own state of mind, then introspection would represent the best description of the approach he not only recommended but regarded as essential.

Krishnamurti's insistence upon this approach was not casual or incidental but comprised a central element of his exposition. He maintained there is no "method" for the direct and immediate observation of one's own state of mind. Any method, any blueprint for psychological observation, would determine or shape the outcome, the phenomena observed. He advocated instead what he called a "choiceless awareness" of the internal landscape, and he insisted that only such a state of mind could achieve true clarity and, ultimately, transformation.

Krishnamurti preferred to call this an art or an approach, rather than a method, but it represents a careful, detailed, fully explicit methodology in the larger sense of that term. This aspect, too, of his overall exposition falls foursquare within the parameters of secular psychology. There is not the slightest hint of any reliance whatsoever on any form of divine or supernatural guidance, and the steady focus of attention is upon the actual, factual reality of ordinary consciousness.

Despite how assiduously secular his stated philosophy was, Krishnamurti did acknowledge another dimension of reality in his personal life. This acknowledgment has no apparent connection with the Theosophical Masters, nor with the out-of-body episodes reported by Mary Lutyens. But late in his life, he allowed to be published a series of notebooks that open a window into his daily experiences and awareness.

Most of the material in these notebooks focuses upon his observations of ordinary consciousness and the natural world. Interspersed with these descriptions, however, are a series of references to another quality or dimension of reality, one which he refers to obliquely as "the other" or "the benediction." This presence is with him intermittently, often at unexpected moments, such as turning a corner in a road on which he is walking. The meaning or quality of this presence is never described in any detail, but its significance for his daily life is unmistakable.

Krishnamurti's life and work encompass several layers or dimensions that are not always easy to reconcile. At the outset of his career was the extraordinary prophecy that he fulfilled to a remarkable degree. A variety of personal experiences recurred throughout his life that cannot be easily accounted for. Superimposed upon this background lies a body of teachings devoid of any reference to otherworldly phenomena, one consisting of descriptions of ordinary consciousness independently verifiable by anyone. This is the record that remains more than two decades after his death and seems unlikely to be augmented to any significant degree for the indefinite future.

The observations contained in this volume shed little light on any mysteries associated with Krishnamurti's personal life. Rather, the evidence assembled here reveals a man wholly devoted to an intention whose meaning is explicit and thoroughly explored in hundreds of hours of recorded dialogues. To be sure, that intention is radical and comprehensive and aims to eradicate the very root of psychological conflict and confusion. But there is nothing mysterious about it, and the realization of this intention depends on nothing other than the unconditioned awareness of one's own state of mind.

That is the work that remains for his schools, and for each individual who has been touched by the man and his work.

Krishnamurti with Oak Grove students.

EPILOGUE

I n the last year of his life, Krishnamurti wondered aloud whether the Oak Grove School would survive after he was gone. His schools in India and in England, he felt, were on a firm foundation and would continue their work into the indefinite future. But he worried that his youngest child, as it were, might not be so stable.

More than two decades after his death, Krishnamurti's apprehensions have not materialized. Oak Grove remains a strong and vital institution, fully engaged in the lives of its students. With an enrollment of some two hundred, the school is at the limit of its physical capacity. It represents a landmark on the educational scene and a member in good standing of the Krishnamurti schools worldwide.

In a private meeting with me just two months before he died, Krishnamurti also raised the question why none of his schools had realized its most basic intention: to produce a new kind of mind, one that is fully self-aware and unconditioned. As a possible explanation, he cited an Indian aphorism: under the banyan tree, nothing grows. After he was gone, he seemed to suggest, the schools might more fully meet their purpose.

On this count, the verdict is less clear-cut. There is no particular evidence that any of his seven schools have generated the kind of consciousness Krishnamurti had in mind. No one has come forth and spoken or written in a manner that would suggest such a transformation. Where an Einstein exists, we expect to see students who have mastered his work and even refined and exceeded it. No one of that kind has appeared in connection with Krishnamurti.

In the case of Oak Grove, therefore, the reality that has emerged lies somewhere between the best and worst that he anticipated. In the language of sports metaphors, the school has neither struck out nor hit a home run. The result that has materialized is perhaps somewhat akin to a ground-rule double: the ball was hit out of the park, but on a bounce.

In order to see what the school has actually become, it may be helpful to put aside its extraordinary intention and examine it strictly on its own terms. If we proceed in that manner, the first and most striking characteristic of the school is the exceptional beauty of its physical setting. In sheer extent, the 150 acres seem almost endless, and the stately oaks, alternating with open fields and wildflowers, are redolent of the beauty and power of nature undisturbed.

The several school buildings—Pavilion, elementary school, secondary school, administration building—were well conceived to harmonize with the land. The widely spaced wooden structures are carefully located for minimal impact upon one another or the property. Their color and manner of construction project a warm, friendly feeling as well as a sense of stability.

But the outward, physical features of the school are merely a vessel for its pedagogical innovations. A visitor to the school on any given day might not notice anything unique or out of the ordinary, but a closer examination would reveal some unusual characteristics. Academic classes are limited in size to twelve or fourteen students. From this follows the possibility of a deeper, more genuine relationship between teacher and student than occurs in most school settings. At Oak Grove, the quality of relationship itself is considered an essential element of the school curriculum.

Closely tied to the quality of relationship is the approach to behavior and discipline. As noted in the present narrative, the school struggled in its early years to develop an approach to discipline that succeeded in maintaining order without recourse to either punishment or reward as techniques for shaping behavior. There is an art to implementing such an approach that depends, in part, on the skill of the teacher and varies somewhat from one classroom to the next. In general, however, Oak Grove succeeds to a remarkable extent in cultivating responsible, sensitive behavior even among its youngest students without recourse to mechanical techniques.

This crucial pedagogical principle extends to the very act of learning. Instruction that is predicated upon the student's achievement of some distant goal represents the prevailing philosophy in most schools and is responsible for much of the discontent experienced by many students. When reward and punishment are both discarded as impediments to real learning, however, it becomes possible for students to approach subjects for the joy of discovery itself. In the language of academicians, learning then is based upon "intrinsic motivation," and there is no longer a basis for the student's sense of alienation from the subject. Without the carrot or the stick, the student may not move as fast, or he or she may move with surprising speed and at times in unexpected directions.

Supplementing these basic features of an Oak Grove education is a variety of other principles that reinforce the cultivation of intelligence. Competition among groups and individuals is discouraged, rather than fostered to spur achievement, as occurs in other settings. Students are not compared with one another as a means of measuring achievement. An extensive program of instruction in the arts—drama, music, photography, ceramics— balances the core academic program.

In addition, the regular and sustained contact with nature is considered a vital element in the student's education, not a mere occasional supplement. The school campus is a source of nature study itself, with an abundance of trees, flowers, gardens, meadows, birds, and other wildlife. Overnight camping trips are a regular feature of the school year. Earth Day is celebrated as a great and festive occasion, with visitors from the community invited to the school and student projects on display.

As interesting as these innovations may be, the test of their success surely lies in the quality of the graduates they produce. Conventional education focuses almost exclusively on academic achievement, and its success is measured in corresponding terms: high school graduation rates, the percentage of graduates that go on to college, and the kind of colleges to which they gain admittance. The success of a school like Oak Grove must include considerations of this kind but not be limited to them. Oak Grove's objectives encompass academic excellence, but its larger intentions must be assessed by other means.

With regard to academic achievement, Oak Grove's record is commendable but not extraordinary. My aim as director was for academic excellence to become a hallmark of the school and a symbol of the superiority of the school's pedagogical philosophy. Nothing of that kind has yet materialized. On the other hand, the school's graduates have a good track record in terms of the number and quality of colleges to which they have gained admission. Oak Grove students have attended each of the dozen campuses in the highly regarded University of California system, in addition to Cornell, Wellesley, Yale, and the Otis College of Art and Design. In general, it seems safe to say that Oak Grove provides an environment in which students may excel academically to whatever extent they choose.

Beyond sheer academic success, the school's achievements are more difficult to measure. There does not exist any standardized test or other objective instrument to assess the degree to which someone is unconditioned. Transformation of consciousness is not a component of the SAT.

Clearly, the school is not a factory for generating reproductions or miniature versions of Krishnamurti. Someone with only a superficial knowledge of the school and its philosophy might be forgiven for speculating that it exists to implement its own form of conditioning—to impress Krishnamurti's philosophy on the minds of its students just as systematically as Catholicism is impressed on the students in parochial schools.

Anyone inclined to this view would surely relinquish it after direct exposure to the actual school and its students. Neither teachers nor students make any effort to emulate Krishnamurti. To do so would be anathema to the freedom from psychological authority at the root of his philosophy.

The nature and effect of an Oak Grove education appear to lie in another direction. There is a model of education that is intended not to pour knowledge into the student but rather to draw out what is already there. The very meaning of the Latin root *educare* ("to lead forth") suggests such a process. Something of this kind may represent the main effect of the school. A student at Oak Grove is perhaps inclined to become more authentically what he or she actually is. In the language of psychologist Abraham Maslow, the school appears to foster self-actualization, rather than conformity to any preconceived model or ideal.

These conclusions are based upon the observation of students and graduates over the course of many years. The effect is apparent in many cases at an early age but even more so as students mature into adulthood. Oak Grove graduates include architects, attorneys, a bicycle mechanic, an organic farmer, yoga teachers, an audio engineer, doctors, computer scientists, photographers, artists, a popular actress, and a few who have returned to teach at Oak Grove. But these people are not necessarily defined by their professions, and they are still unfolding their potentiality.

Whether the school will ever achieve its ultimate aim remains an open question. Deep and large intentions perhaps require a corresponding period of maturation before they come to fruition.

What can be said with confidence is that the soil has been prepared, the seed has been planted, and some brightly colored flowers have emerged. No external boundaries or impediments are blocking the school's development, and its future bears watching. In the fullness of time, its innermost nature will be revealed.

ACKNOWLEDGMENTS

I t takes a village to raise a child, and it takes another kind of community to give birth to a book. My sense of indebtedness is broad and deep.

Every writer seeks encouragement as well as practical assistance, and no one gave me more of both than Adelle Chabelski. Her appreciation for the value of the work was instrumental in its seeing the light of day. It was she who made the connection with Quest Books, and Quest, in turn—as Adelle accurately foresaw—turned out to be the ideal home for this volume.

Sharron Dorr, the publications manager at Quest, has been a delightful and steady partner throughout the publication process. Among other things, she selected a superb editor for the manuscript. Joanne Asala fine-tuned the text with exceptional care and skill, and she put up with a rather demanding author with an abundance of grace and good humor.

Many friends read the manuscript at various stages of its evolution and offered constructive commentary. My sister Leanne

Grove and her friend Clare Mellow were among the first of these, and their early suggestions had a lasting effect. Patricia Papernow provided the most copious set of comments I received as well as an insightful overall perspective. Judith Mostyn read a portion of the draft and offered appreciative support.

The views of Michael Krohnen and Michael Lommel were informed by their familiarity with the teachings of Krishnamurti. My dear friend Michael Krohnen was especially generous with his criticism, including his doubt that any publisher would invest in a work with such limited appeal.

Suza Francina and Marilyn Mosley Gordanier each offered unique perspectives on the manuscript and cogent recommendations.

Friedrich Grohe and his team were very supportive and largely responsible for the inclusion of the chapter on the Insight Curriculum. Jurgen Brandt wrote a short essay in response to the manuscript, one that I greatly appreciated. Claudia Herr examined every word and phrase with an eagle eye and made numerous corrections. Raman Patel offered good counsel and friendly encouragement.

Mary Zimbalist read a draft of the manuscript just a few months before her death. She kindly wrote a short letter of support, including a couple of factual corrections.

Mark Lee discovered half a dozen errors in the text that everyone else had overlooked. I am most grateful for his close attention as well as for his words of approval of the manuscript as a whole.

As much as I appreciate all the help I received, any mistakes of fact or interpretation that survived into the final draft must remain, of course, my sole responsibility.

Krishnamurti at a public talk in San Diego, March 7, 1974.

THE INTENT OF THE OAK GROVE SCHOOL

[Author's note: Krishnamurti composed this document several months before the school opened in 1975.]

It is becoming more and more important in a world that is degenerating that there should be a place, an oasis, where one can learn a way of living that is whole, sane, and holy. Education in the modern world has been concerned with the cultivation of memory and its skills. This has been a process in which information is passed from the teacher to the taught, the leader to the follower, bringing about a superficial and mechanical way of life. In this, there is little human relationship.

Surely a school is a place where one learns about the totality of life, the wholeness of life. It is a place where both the teacher and the taught explore academic subjects as well as their own thinking and their own activities. They come to see how their conditioning distorts their thinking. This conditioning is the self to which such tremendous and absurd importance is given. The awareness of this brings freedom from conditioning and its misery. It is only in freedom that learning can take place. Both the teacher and the student are conditioned. In this school, it is the responsibility of the teacher through discussion to explore with the student the implications of conditioning and thus end it.

A school is a place where one learns both the importance of knowledge and its irrelevance. It is a place where one learns to observe the world not from any particular point of view or conclusion. One learns to look at the whole of man's endeavor, his search for beauty, his search for truth and a way of living that is not a contradiction between conclusion and action. It is a place where both the teacher and the taught learn a way of life in which conflict ends. Conflict is the very essence of violence.

It is here one learns the importance of relationship which is not based on attachment and possession. It is in the school one must learn about the movement of thought, love, and death, for all this is the whole of life.

Religion has become a romantic, authoritarian refuge of superstition and fancy. Religion is none of these things. Education is concerned with learning the true significance of the religious mind. It is only this mind that can gather all its energy to live a complete life without fragmentation. This whole movement of living brings about naturally a psychological revolution, and from this comes a totally different social order.

The school is concerned with freedom and order. Freedom is not the expression of one's own desire and choice. That inevitably will lead to disorder. Freedom of choice is not freedom, though it may appear so. Order is not conformity or imitation. Order comes with the insight that choice denies freedom. Where there is a division between idea and action, there is conflict and confusion. To perceive is to act.

The school will give importance to the cultivation of knowledge, the real understanding of its function, and go beyond knowledge to a transformation of consciousness. When all this takes place, a new human being will emerge who will affect the consciousness of the world.

J. Krishnamurti
March 1, 1975
Ojai, California

THE INTENT OF THE OAK GROVE SCHOOL (REVISED)

[Author's note: As one of several changes that occurred in the spring of 1984, the statement of intent underwent a careful review and significant modification. Several of those responsible for the school participated in this process, but Krishnamurti gave close attention to every word before he approved of the final document.]

I t is becoming more and more important in a world that is destructive and degenerating that there should be a place, an oasis, where one can learn a way of living that is whole, sane, and intelligent. Education in the modern world has been concerned with the cultivation not of intelligence, but of intellect, of memory and its skills. In this process, little occurs beyond passing information from the teacher to the taught, the leader to the follower, bringing about a superficial and mechanical way of life. In this, there is little human relationship.

Surely a school is a place where one learns about the totality, the wholeness of life. Academic excellence is absolutely necessary, but a school includes much more than that. It is a place where both the teacher and the taught explore not only the outer world, the world of knowledge, but also their own thinking, their own behavior. From this, they begin to discover their own conditioning and how it distorts their thinking. This conditioning is the self to which such tremendous and cruel importance is given. Freedom from conditioning and its misery begins with this awareness. It is only in such freedom that true learning can take place. In this school, it is the responsibility of the teacher to sustain with the student a careful exploration into the implications of conditioning and thus end it.

A school is a place where one learns the importance of knowledge and its limitations. It is a place where one learns to observe the world not from any particular point of view or conclusion. One learns to look at the whole of man's endeavor, his search for beauty, his search for truth and for a way of living without conflict. Conflict is the very essence of violence. So far, education has not been concerned with this, but in this school, our intent is to understand actuality and its action without any preconceived ideals, theories, or beliefs which bring about a contradictory attitude toward existence.

The school is concerned with freedom and order. Freedom is not the expression of one's own desire, choice, or self-interest. That inevitably leads to disorder. Freedom of choice is not freedom, though it may appear so; nor is order conformity or imitation. Order can only come with the insight that to choose is itself the denial of freedom.

In school, one learns the importance of relationship, which is not based on attachment or possession. It is here one can learn about the movement of thought, love, and death, for all this is our life.

From the ancient of times, man has sought something beyond the materialistic world, something immeasurable, something sacred. It is the intent of this school to inquire into this possibility.

This whole movement of inquiry into knowledge, into oneself, into the possibility of something beyond knowledge, brings about naturally a psychological revolution, and from this comes, inevitably, a totally different order in human relationship, which is society. The intelligent understanding of all this can bring about a profound change in the consciousness of mankind.

RESPONSIBILITY AND THE COMMON GROUND

AT THE OAK GROVE SCHOOL

[Author's note: In the spring of 1980, Krishnamurti asked me to summarize the essence of a series of meetings that he had conducted with the school faculty and administration. This is the document I composed, which the trustees of the Krishnamurti Foundation of America accepted and approved. Krishnamurti inserted the sentence in the first paragraph that begins with "The essence of the common ground."]

The Oak Grove School has areas of individual function and responsibility—such as teaching science to a group of students—and it has a common ground. The common ground is the necessity to bring about in both students and educators the capacity for learning—the capacity to live intelligent lives. The essence of the common ground is to bring about good human beings. The areas of individual responsibility are to the common ground as the school's buildings are to the land: the individual areas lie in and on the common ground; they are joined together by it; from it, they arise. On the common ground, all those responsible for the school—director, staff, trustees—have the responsibility to meet.

The Oak Grove School is part of a larger enterprise; it exists under the auspices of the Krishnamurti Foundation of America, a nonprofit charitable trust administered solely by the several trustees of the foundation. The trustees are ultimately responsible for all foundation activities both within and outside of the school. Within the school, however, the trustees' responsibility is shared.

Where responsibility is shared, the possibility for misunderstanding may arise. The statements that follow are enunciated here in an effort to minimize that possibility.

1. As the buildings are to the land, the areas of individual responsibility are rooted in the common ground. Together, the individual and common areas constitute the school as a whole. A member of staff is responsible both for an individual area and for the common ground. In addition, the staff member acquires, through the common ground, a degree of responsibility for the individual areas of other members of staff; one is responsible for the area of another to the degree that that area affects the common ground. In this way, the part becomes responsible for the whole.

2. The director's responsibility for the whole, by contrast, is unqualified (except by the responsibility of the trustees). He is also responsible to the trustees and to keep them fully informed regarding school matters.

One of the director's functions is to communicate effectively with those responsible for the parts of the school, for it is largely through him that they become cognizant of the whole; he is to them as the hub to the spokes of a wheel. It is his responsibility not only to communicate with them, but also to facilitate their communication with one another: it is his job to help them achieve general consensus regarding decision or actions that significantly affect the whole, such as the selection and dismissal of students and staff. Whether in the presence or in the absence of a consensus, however, the director alone is authorized by the trustees to act authoritatively on behalf of the whole.

3. All responsibility for foundation monies, including funds raised for the school or designated for school use, lies in the hands of the trustees.

The common ground of the school is made fertile by passionate commitment. Passionate commitment to a shared responsibility implies several things: it implies the capacity to observe in oneself the impediments to cooperation; it implies the capacity to distinguish one's personal perspective from a view of the whole; it implies the capacity to listen.

APPENDIX 4

STATEMENT TO THE TRUSTEES
OF THE KRISHNAMURTI
FOUNDATION OF AMERICA

[Author's note: In February 1984, a substantial number of parents of students enrolled in the school signed this letter addressed to the trustees of the KFA.]

February 1984

We, the undersigned parents and guardians of children at the Oak Grove School, hereby wish to make the following statement with regard to the school, its educational administration, and its relationship to our children.

We have all brought here, from many parts of the world, our families and children, often at considerable physical and economic sacrifice, in the spirit of finding a truly "new" kind of education. We hoped, of course, that the school would attempt to instill an educational approach more or less grounded in the teachings of Mr. Krishnamurti. We do feel that a beautiful physical presence has been provided at the Oak Grove, with its elegant structures interlaced among the oak trees, flowers, and gardens, and surrounded by the soft hills of the valley. We are very appreciative of the commitment and dedication that brought this setting about. Also, we wish to express our full support and appreciation of the teachers at the school, who, having come here in much the same spirit as the parents, exhibit excellence in character and commitment as educators, as well as individuals, in the spirit of a school associated with Mr. Krishnamurti.

Please understand that the writing of this letter was not undertaken lightly. Over the years, many parents have attempted to communicate their concerns to the administrative officers, often to no avail. Many parents have spent long hours exploring their concerns with the teachers and among themselves. We have often examined what would be the most intelligent and caring approach to resolving this dilemma concerning our common and pervasive dissatisfaction with the educational environment being created for our children at the Oak Grove School.

We now appeal to you, only after it has become certain to us that this problem cannot be resolved by the school's present educational administrators (i.e., the school board and the school committee). In fact, it is clear that a powerful group of the school's administrators themselves, as well as the administrative structure and the administrative style, *are the problem*.

We are very concerned with the absence of educational clarity at the school. The unfortunate and continuing turnover among the staff, the ongoing loss of student enrollment, and the breakdown of a spirit of "common enterprise" are serious concerns to us. And, of course, we are well aware how many explanations can be offered for the causes of these concerns, all generally supporting the positions of those who voice them. With this difficulty in mind, however, we do feel that the present educational administrative structure is both functionally inappropriate and unrepresentative of a large body of both parents and staff, as well as the educational environment described during enlistment of new students and in the promotional materials for the school. This body of parents has, perhaps due to "political" disinterest, inarticulateness, absence of a proper forum, as well as personal respect for those in the administration, remained generally silent and supportive.

It is important to emphasize that the dissatisfaction we are expressing is due primarily to our complete loss of confidence and trust in the present educational administration. We are not interested in imposing our opinions on you, nor do we seek a democratic approach with equal representation through all phases of the school's operation. We do feel, however, that we (the parents) no longer experience a spirit of openness and cooperation. We ask that you carefully and deeply consider that the present educational administration is unsatisfactory.

The keynote of the school's administrative *style* is authority. The use of authority to deal with issues or problems is preferred to problem solving through cooperation. If a problem is perceived as an obstacle to overcome, the resulting action is to suppress or "gloss over" the problem. This attitude tends to lead to making a rule or regulation by an authoritative body and then *imposing* it. This is usually described as "necessary" for practical efficiency by those presently responsible.

There should be no surprise, then, that the campus at the Oak Grove is certainly not free from an atmosphere of repressed fear, frustration, and genuine and unrelieved bewilderment. The *impression* received is that those most "responsible" are apparently fearful of students, parents, and teachers. This results in an increasing need for tighter control, which further undermines good communication and effective education. Misperception is inevitable in such an environment.

The educational administrative *structure* also lends itself to the types of problems experienced at the school. When several persons, of varying capacities and educational attitudes, are given power to dictate to others (including the teachers themselves), then it seems unfair to turn around and blame them for using that power.

This prevailing style of authoritative interaction can be avoided by a style *and* structure founded on cooperative understanding and trust. Such an alternative to this authoritative approach requires integrity, commitment, and administrative skill from one (or those) most responsible for the day-to-day operations of a school. An authentic and genuine care and concern for the needs of others is very important, as well as a capacity to have genuine, accurate, and meaningful communication with others. These qualities, which help bring about understanding between all concerned, are now absent from the general atmosphere at the Oak Grove School. The qualities you might select in your administrator(s) are an educational attitude (and background) reflective of an approach suggested by Mr. Krishnamurti (free of coercion, strife, dogma, fear, etc.), love and respect for children, the skills to effectively communicate this attitude to all concerned without creating distance and fragmentation, a compassionate openness to others, and a commitment to bringing about a "new" kind of education.

The Oak Grove School is in crisis. We are literally begging you to make a real and effective change in this serious matter. We hope you will be responsive to this plea. We, as you, wish to support this enterprise far into the future.

Thank you.

Respectfully,
(44 signatures)

APPENDIX 5

TOWARD A COMPREHENSIVE, COHERENT CURRICULUM

[Author's note: In the summer of 1985, I wrote this essay intended to serve as the foundation for a new curriculum, one that would be, in a sense, unconditioned and consonant with the deeper purposes of the school. The essay was published in a journal of the Krishnamurti schools.]

Of course, the intention of these schools embraces much more than the sum of the knowledge we wish to convey. Even within the field of knowledge, we hope the child will discover a great deal for himself, apart from whatever information we wish to prescribe. We also intend that the child should grasp the limitations of knowledge, and perhaps even find out what it means to live in freedom from the known. But the very breadth and depth of our intention ought not to incline us to neglect that there does remain a substantial fund of knowledge we wish to impart to the children. This quantity of prescribed knowledge is called here curriculum.

Among the qualities that seem desirable in a general curriculum for school children are comprehensiveness and coherence. This essay proposes that at the core of any curriculum that can be considered comprehensive, there ought to lie an articulated vision—a description, a portrait, a map—of the whole of what is: that is, a vision of the universe, in which the fundamental phenomena of the universe (matter, life, mind) are displayed, not only as whole in their own right, but also in their relationship to one another. A preliminary sketch of one such articulated vision follows. It is offered not only to be examined on its own terms, as to whether it is an accurate portrait of reality, but also, and for present purposes more importantly, it is offered simply as an example of how such a vision might possibly look. What is important in any such vision is that it be *comprehensive*, show all the major, known varieties of phenomena in the universe, and that it specify, make explicit, the *relationships* among those phenomena; for it is only by virtue of these relationships that the universe is, in fact, one.

The vision offered here proposes that the world around us actually consists of three universes, three distinguishable realms or dimensions, three semi-autonomous realities in the overall fabric of what is. They are autonomous, inasmuch as each dimension represents a unique set of phenomena, and of underlying principles accounting for those phenomena; yet they are only semi-autonomous, since the dimensions arise organically from one another, as the tree from the earth.

These three realms are as follows:

(1) a physical dimension of space and time, matter and energy, of tangible and measurable phenomena of mathematical predictability, from which arises a new order of matter and energy;

(2) a biological universe, in which the evolution of structures of ever-increasing complexity implies a new set of operating principles, by which has arisen yet a new kind of actuality;

(3) a psychological universe, the mind of man, in which conflict and confusion are paradoxically mixed with intelligence, all of which again requires new explanatory insights.

This proposal is presented in greater detail below, with special attention to (a) why each "dimension" is to be understood as a whole in its own right and (b) the relationship of each dimension to the others.

The delineation of these three realms in no way denies their inseparability; on the contrary, it emphasizes it by displaying the way each is connected with the other. And the connections described here in no way exclude the possibility of other, perhaps more profound, connections. Thus, someone may propose that life not only represents a new organization of matter, but that it is, in fact, the expression and manifestation of the inward essence of matter; or that mind is the expression and manifestation of the inward essence of life, or even of matter.

Such a vision or map of all reality becomes the blueprint for the curriculum, or at least for the core sequence of the curriculum. Other subjects, peripheral to the core, are then understood by both teacher and taught as special excursions into critical areas of the map. Learning to write, for example, would be considered in this curriculum in terms of its place in the overall development of mind (specifically as the externalization of abstract, conceptual thought into a visual channel). Physical education is an interesting blend of physical mechanics, physiological principles, and psychological responses. Like any map, this one need not operate as a set of instructions; rather, it is available as an organizing framework, indicating the territory to be covered and showing the relationship of a given topic to others; but it is quite open-ended regarding instructional questions of approach and sequence.

An articulated vision of the whole at the core of the curriculum would seem to confer certain advantages. Primarily, it would offer an antidote to fragmentation, to the ubiquitous tendency for curriculum to degenerate into a buffet of disconnected subjects. By having the whole of what is at its center, the curriculum might have the opportunity to become whole itself, that is, for its parts to have coherence, order, intrinsic internal relationship. Such a curriculum might help bring coherence to the child's entire experience of the school; and, if adopted by several schools, might further the intention of those schools to act as one.

The following vision, or map, need not be accepted as an accurate portrait of reality in order for this proposition to remain intact: that *some* comprehensive view of the whole, made explicit for general inspection, is indispensable to the construction of a sound curriculum. Corrections and elaborations, either of the following vision or of the foregoing proposition, would be most welcome; this is a work in progress.

I. THE PHYSICAL UNIVERSE

The universe as we know it consists fundamentally of a physical dimension of space and time, of matter and energy, of observable, measurable, mathematically describable phenomena. Except at the subatomic level (and possibly even there), this physical universe appears to be fully deterministic.

Although our understanding of physical reality has grown enormously in recent centuries, the history of that development makes clear that what we accept as knowledge today may be modified or even overturned by tomorrow's discoveries. Moreover, although the physical realm may be the most basic level of reality that we know, its existence is itself a profound mystery. Why should anything physically exist at all? Is there a deeper, more fundamental, yet ineffable order of existence, a dimension of mathematics, or of mind, that both underlies and expresses itself in physical reality? We don't really know; our knowledge is (and ever will be) limited, embedded in the vast sea of the unknown.

II. THE BIOLOGICAL UNIVERSE

Matter is at the basis of life; there is no organism without a body. However, life represents a special refinement, an unusual organization of matter, a new order that enables new phenomena to take place, and that entails new principles underlying these phenomena.

What is unique about life as an arrangement of matter is that it is so designed as to allow the introduction of energy into that system (the organism) and the incorporation of that energy into the internal functioning of the system. The sun is the motor that runs the whole biosphere, the global ecosystem. The miracle of life begins—logically, if not chronologically—with photosynthesis, i.e., with the moment that a collection of otherwise inorganic molecules becomes so arranged as to enable them to capture radiant energy from the sun and to convert that energy into a form usable by those molecules to sustain their own organization.

The biosphere is the distribution and interrelationships of all living things on earth. Of the immense diversity of organisms on earth, there are those who obtain their energy directly from the sun and those who obtain their energy indirectly from the sun by consuming other organisms.

How did all this diversity arise? What is the origin of the existence of *species* of plants and animals? Evolution as the fundamental explanatory principle of the manifestations of life. Molecular basis of evolution: the selfish gene.

III. The Psychological Universe

Perhaps it was the nature of mammalian life in the trees, with its dual demand for excellent bifocal vision combined with extreme manual dexterity, that stimulated the latest mushrooming of cells in the evolution of the brain. Whatever the evolutionary impetus, the human brain appears to represent a quantum leap in the overall development of living things, bringing into full flower a new dimension of existence—mind—with phenomena and principles that arise from and yet qualitatively transcend those of organic life, just as life both arises from and transcends the matter and energy of the physical universe.

The essence of mind is intelligence. What is the nature of this quality called intelligence in which mankind represents a quantum leap? Intelligence has three attributes or factors: memory, logic, and insight. Each took a quantum leap with the appearance of man, but of the three, memory appears to play the dominant, largest role: in origin of civilization (calendars, written records, etc.), in development of culture, in science and technology.

In the course of the development of human intelligence, however, a deep-seated error appears to have entered in. The simple fact that man is everywhere at war with himself and his environment is surely symptomatic of something gone wrong; mankind appears to have taken a wrong turn. Where? In what way?

One explanation that has been put forth is that man, with his immensely expanded capacity for memory (knowledge, thought), has begun to misuse this tool, particularly insofar as he has applied it to himself. The sense of personal identity—which may exist in some primitive form in animals, but which really blossoms and crystallizes in man—is, in essence, simply the individual's memory of himself, though it is not experienced as memory, but rather as a living, abiding entity, the me. This sense of psychological identity, of a self at the center of existence, introduces a fundamental division in the very consciousness of man; and psychological division always leads to conflict. Thus, the whole panorama of human history.

Though each regards himself as unique, human beings everywhere are, in fact, much more alike than different: all suffer; all experience fear, desire, loneliness, etc.; all are caught in trying to become something they are not. Thus, you are the world.

APPENDIX 6

THE APPROACH TO EDUCATION AT OAK GROVE

[Author's note: Among the multitude of files of letters, papers, and documents that I accumulated during my years at Oak Grove, there is a short piece of particular interest whose origin I no longer remember clearly. I believe it is a statement I elicited from Krishnamurti over the course of two or three lunchtime conversations. It represents a partial answer to the kind of question I attempted to explore at Oak Grove: how exactly the overarching principles of Krishnamurti's philosophy applied to the concrete actualities of daily life in the classroom.

The language of the document consists of a blend of his manner of expression and mine. The substance, however, is very characteristic of his views and not the kind of thing I would have composed. At the end of the typewritten document, there appears in my handwriting a notation in pen: "JK/dm 5/12/84." I take this to indicate I considered it to be essentially a piece dictated by him to me, perhaps with some interpolation of my own language and phrasing.]

At the foundation of the approach to education at Oak Grove, there is discipline. Fundamentally, etymologically, the word *discipline* means, not conformity, but to learn. Discipline begins with the elementary activities of daily living. It begins with learning, for example, to speak properly: to speak slowly, to enunciate, to use language correctly, to use appropriate forms of address, to attend to one's tone of voice. It includes learning to dress and to keep one's hair with sensitivity and good taste. It extends to the way in which one eats, as well as to the food one selects: healthful, balanced, and (except in extremity) without taking the lives of animals.

The discipline of learning, of watching one's own behavior in daily activity, is the beginning of order in those activities; and that watching, and that order, may then move inwardly, as it were, to the responses, the reactions, the states of mind that produce the outward behavior. In this school, it is the vocation of the teacher to cultivate such discipline in his own life as well as in the lives of his students.

If discipline means to learn, what is the quality of mind that is capable of learning? Attention is the essence of learning. Attention means hearing, listening; hearing with the ear as well as "behind" the ear. Attention is a natural function of the nervous system; it cannot be so much cultivated as denied. It is denied when the brain, or mind, is occupied, occupied with a problem, a goal, or with any prolonged particular object of attention.

Entertainment, which means literally "to hold between," is whatever we allow to hold our attention between occupations; as such, it is itself a form of occupation. Even interest is a form of occupation: one can only be interested *in* something; therefore, interest is always partial and dependent on its object; there is no interest *per se*. Attention is the quality of mind that is occupied with nothing partial, and therefore with nothing at all. A mind that is occupied with nothing at all is in a state of leisure.

The state of leisure, of a mind that is quiet, unoccupied, attentive, cannot be brought about through any technique or method. Method entails motive, interest, direction; attention is the absence of these. The attentive teacher will naturally notice attentiveness in his students and will protect and encourage it as it appears. If it can be sustained, the students' attention will, in due course, turn by itself toward the teacher, and classroom instruction may proceed.

What is the attentive teacher's right relationship, right response, to *in*attention in his students? Inattention is mindless activity, activity without awareness, whether activity of the body, or of the tongue, or of the brain. Neither psychological nor electronic contrivances (reward and punishment, computers) can break down the barriers to attention; they only substitute new barriers.

Faced with inattention, the teacher may perhaps begin class with a moment or two of silence—unless that request will be met with resistance and so become another barrier. In such a case, as class begins, the teacher may simply sit attentively, quietly, by himself. Such attentiveness (if it is real!) will soon be observed by members of the class; and by that observation, it will communicate itself. It becomes the task of the teacher, therefore, to set aside every form of pressure, of interest, of occupation, in order to come in himself upon that state of free attention, that quality of leisure, only in which learning can occur.

From the ancient of times, man has sought something beyond the materialistic world. It is the intent of this school to inquire into that possibility.

SOURCES AND REFERENCES

The source for all the quotations that appear in Chapters 1 and 2 is the first volume of Mary Lutyens's biography of Krishnamurti: *Krishnamurti: The Years of Awakening* (New York: Farrar, Strauss and Giroux, 1975). This material is copyright 1975 Krishnamurti Foundation of America.

Excerpts from Krishnamurti's dialogues with Oak Grove parents, teachers, and staff appear in the introductory quotation and in Chapters 3 and 8. Verbatim transcriptions of these dialogues were prepared by me in the years after I left the school. By "verbatim" is meant that the transcripts record literally every word and syllable exactly as they occur in the recorded dialogues. Only punctuation is added in order to make the material readable on the printed page. For purposes of this volume, however, the excerpts that appear here were lightly edited to make them more accessible to a general audience. This material is copyright Krishnamurti Foundation Trust, Ltd., in England.

The quotation from Aldous Huxley that appears in Chapter

15 is from the foreword to *The First and Last Freedom* (New York: Harper and Brothers, 1954).

The two path-breaking papers published by David Bohm in 1952 (mentioned in Chapter 15) are as follows:

"A Suggested Interpretation of the Quantum Theory in Terms of Hidden Variables I," *Physical Review*, vol. 85 (1952), pp. 166–179.

"A Suggested Interpretation of the Quantum Theory in Terms of Hidden Variables II," *Physical Review*, vol. 85 (1952), pp. 180–193.

Readers interested in understanding more about student misconceptions in the sciences, as discussed in Chapter 16, may consult Chapter 4, "Student Misconceptions in Biology," in *Mapping Biology Knowledge* by Kathleen M. Fisher, James H. Wandersee, and David E. Moody (Dordrecht, the Netherlands: Kluwer [now Springer], 2000).

BIBLIOGRAPHIC

ESSAY

Krishnamurti's appointed biographer was Mary Lutyens, who examined his life in four volumes. An earlier book composed by Mary Lutyens's mother, Lady Emily Lutyens, was entitled *Candles in the Sun* (J. B. Lippincott Company, 1957). This was a firsthand account of Krishnamurti's life as an adolescent and a young man, as well as of prominent members of the Theosophical Society who raised and nurtured him.

Through her mother, Mary Lutyens was friends with Krishnamurti and his brother Nitya from the days of her childhood. She composed her own recollections of those early days, *To Be Young* (Rupert Hart-Davis, 1959), as well as biographies of John Ruskin and of her father, the distinguished architect Sir Edwin Lutyens, before she began to write about Krishnamurti. The four volumes of her biography of him are as follows:

Krishnamurti: The Years of Awakening (Farrar, Straus and Giroux, 1975) covers the period from his birth in 1895 until 1933, a few years after he dissolved the Order of the Star in the East.

Krishnamurti: The Years of Fulfillment (Farrar, Straus and Giroux, 1983) covers the period from 1933 until 1980.

Krishnamurti: The Open Door (Farrar, Straus and Giroux, 1988) covers the final years of his life and the circumstances surrounding his death in 1986.

Krishnamurti: His Life and Death (St. Martin's Press, 1990) is a final summary work that reviews his entire life in a single volume, with a more narrow focus than the previous books on the essential nature of Krishnamurti's consciousness.

Of these four volumes, the last is by far the best. The first two books are detailed, factual accounts of a story that is fascinating in its own right, but they are rendered in a rather dry and detached manner that fails to bring its subject to life. The more compressed nature of the final book, as well as its focus on the question "Who or what was Krishnamurti?" makes for a more compelling narrative.

An alternative account of Krishnamurti's life is *Krishnamurti: A Biography* by Pupul Jayakar (Harper and Row, 1986). Jayakar was a major intellectual figure, high governmental official, and close friend and confidante of Prime Minister Indira Gandhi. She was a devoted student of Krishnamurti's work and a prominent member of the Krishnamurti Foundation India. Her book displays her formidable talents as a writer and a thinker and her deep appreciation for the man and his work.

A more recent biography is *Star in the East: Krishnamurti—The Invention of a Messiah* by Roland Vernon (Sentient Publications, 2002). Although the author promises an account of "water-tight impartiality," in fact he presents a somewhat distorted view, one that emphasizes Krishnamurti's early association with Theosophy and largely overlooks the gulf between Krishnamurti's stated philosophy and Theosophical principles and beliefs.

Among the earliest memoirs of Krishnamurti (apart from *Candles in the Sun*) is *Krishnamurti: The Reluctant Messiah* by screenwriter Sidney Field (Paragon House, 1989). This volume describes the author's interactions with Krishnamurti as a young man, including their mutual acquaintance with various Hollywood personalities.

A few years later, there appeared a pejorative memoir entitled *Lives in the Shadow with J. Krishnamurti* (Addison Wesley Publishing Company, 1993)—the title is a play on *Candles in the Sun*—by Radha Rajagopal Sloss, the daughter of Krishnamurti's longtime financial manager. Sloss reveals Krishnamurti's affair of many years with her mother Rosalind, which began after her parents had ceased living together. Sloss uses this revelation as a springboard to disparage Krishnamurti's personality and behavior in a variety of ways.

Although her central allegation is true, Sloss's book is riddled with distortions and inaccuracies. These are dissected in careful detail by Mary Lutyens in the small volume *Krishnamurti and the Rajagopals* (Krishnamurti Foundation of America, 1996). This is the best of Mary Lutyens's work, as she contradicts Sloss with absolute rigor and an abundance of evidence, in a style of writing evidently fueled by a cold but controlled fury.

A delightful, entertaining, and well-composed memoir is *The Kitchen Chronicles: 1001 Lunches with J. Krishnamurti* (Edwin House Publishing, 1997) by Michael Krohnen. Krohnen was Krishnamurti's chef in Ojai from 1975 to 1986, and his affectionate observations are detailed and illuminating.

Also brought out by Edwin House is *A Vision of the Sacred: My Personal Journey with Krishnamurti* by Sunanda Patwardhan (1999). This work couples descriptions of direct interactions with

Krishnamurti with insights and reflections upon the meaning of his teachings.

Centered Self without Being Self-Centered: Remembering Krishnamurti (Morning Light Press, 2003) by Ravi Ravindra is a philosophy professor's scholarly reflections upon the meaning of Krishnamurti's work, as informed and amplified by numerous conversations between the two men.

The Beauty of the Mountain: Memories of J. Krishnamurti (Friedrich Grohe, 1991) by Friedrich Grohe is a charming and vivid record of the author's friendship with Krishnamurti during the last years of his life, adorned with the author's beautiful nature photographs.

The best way to gain access to the actual teachings of Krishnamurti is by means of the many audio and video recordings of his talks and dialogues, available through the Krishnamurti Foundation of America. For those who prefer the written word or a more complete selection, his teachings are preserved in dozens of volumes published throughout his lifetime. Anyone new to his work would do well, in my judgment, to choose a book published after 1960 consisting of a set of his public talks, rather than selected excerpts from his talks, or his written work. Among the many books of this kind is *The Flight of the Eagle* (Harper and Row, 1971). Also in this vein is *Last Talks at Saanen, 1985* (Harper and Row, 1986), a handsome volume that includes many photographs of Krishnamurti and of the Saanen gathering.

Krishnamurti kept a series of diaries recording his personal observations and experiences for occasional periods during the last two or three decades of his life. These works dovetail, in many respects, with his stated philosophy, but they also include material that he never alluded to from the public platform. Vivid and intensely felt descriptions of nature and observations of ordinary consciousness are interspersed with his awareness of another kind or dimension of mind or reality, which he refers to as "the other" or "this benediction."

These more private ruminations and recollections are contained in three volumes. The longest and most profound of these is *Krishnamurti's Notebook* (Victor Golancz Ltd., 1976). *Krishnamurti's Journal* (Victor Golancz Ltd., 1982) and *Krishnamurti to Himself* (Harper and Row, 1987) are shorter, somewhat more accessible works with similarly personal observations.

David Bohm's intellectual interests and pursuits were so wide ranging that they must present a challenge to any biographer. So far, only David Peat has attempted the task, and he did so with only marginal success. *Infinite Potential: The Life and Times of David Bohm* (Addison-Wesley, 1997) is a competent account of Bohm's early life and of his contributions to quantum physics, but it falls rather short in its effort to incorporate the meaning and significance of Bohm's relationship with the teachings and personality of Krishnamurti.

Fortunately, many of Bohm's dialogues with Krishnamurti were recorded and published and so do not depend upon any third party for explication. Among the several volumes of this kind is *The Ending of Time* (Harper and Row, 1985). A number of video recordings of their dialogues are also available through the KFA.

Bohm's unique voice and original expression of the problems and dynamics of the psychological field are preserved mainly as transcripts of dialogues he conducted with groups of twenty to fifty observers and participants. Perhaps the best of these is *Thought as a System* (Routledge, 1992). A related range of topics is explored in a collection of essays in *On Creativity* (Routledge, 1998), edited by Lee Nichol (a name that may be familiar to readers of the present volume).

Bohm's scientific publications are not exclusively technical, and he made some effort to make aspects of his work accessible to a wider audience. His exceptional gift for lucid exposition is on full display in the classic *Causality and Chance in Modern Physics* (D. Van Nostrand Company, Inc., 1957). A deeper, more mature, and more comprehensive account of his views of physical reality and its relationship to consciousness is given in *Wholeness and the Implicate Order* (Routledge and Kegan Paul, 1980)—arguably among the foremost contributions to intellectual discourse of the twentieth century.

PHOTO CREDITS

Chapter 5: (Photographer unknown.) Copyright Krishnamurti Foundation of America.

Chapter 6: Photograph by Rita Zampese. Copyright Rita Zampese.

Chapter 7: (Photographer unknown.) Copyright Krishnamurti Foundation of America.

Chapter 8: Photograph by Mary Zimbalist. Copyright Krishnamurti Foundation of America.

Chapter 9: Photograph by Asit Chandmal. Copyright Krishnamurti Foundation of America.

Chapter 10: Photograph by Michael Mendizza. Copyright Michael Mendizza. Reproduced by permission of Krishnamurti Foundation of America.

Chapter 11: (Photographer unknown.) Copyright Krishnamurti Foundation of America.

Chapter 12: Photograph by Mark Edwards. Copyright Krishnamurti Foundation Trust, England.

Chapter 13: Photograph courtesy of Krishnamurti Foundations.

Chapter 14: Photograph by Mark Edwards. Copyright Krishnamurti Foundation Trust, England.

Chapter 15: Photograph by Mark Edwards. Copyright Krishnamurti Foundation Trust, England.

Chapter 16: Photograph by Michael Mendizza. Copyright Michael Mendizza. Reproduced by permission of Krishnamurti Foundation of America.

Chapter 17: Photograph by Ziegler. Copyright Krishnamurti Foundation of America.

Epilogue: Photograph by Michael Mendizza. Copyright Michael Mendizza. Reproduced by permission of Krishnamurti Foundation of America.

Appendix: Photograph by Mary Zimbalist. Copyright Krishnamurti Foundation of America.

INDEX

Bold type indicates illustrations.

Quest Books
encourages open-minded inquiry into
world religions, philosophy, science, and the arts
in order to understand the wisdom of the ages,
respect the unity of all life, and help people explore
individual spiritual self-transformation.

Its publications are generously supported by
The Kern Foundation,
a trust committed to Theosophical education.

Quest Books is the imprint of
the Theosophical Publishing House,
a division of the Theosophical Society in America.
For information about programs, literature,
on-line study, membership benefits, and international centers,
see www.theosophical.org
or call 800-669-1571 or (outside the U.S.) 630-668-1571.

To order books or a complete Quest catalog,
call 800-669-9425 or (outside the U.S.) 630-665-0130.

Related Quest Titles

Commentaries on Living, by J. Krishnamurti

The Inner Life of J. Krishnamurti, by Aryel Sanat

Krishnamurti: Two Birds on One Tree, by Ravi Ravindra

To order books or a complete Quest catalog,
call 800-669-9425 or (outside the U.S.) 630-665-0130.